THE
DIVINE HOURS™
POCKET EDITION

Psalm 119:164

Seven times each day I praise you for the justice of your decrees.

THE
DIVINE HOURS™

POCKET EDITION

Compiled and with an Introduction by
Phyllis Tickle

OXFORD
UNIVERSITY PRESS
2007

OXFORD
UNIVERSITY PRESS

Oxford University Press, Inc., publishes works that further
Oxford University's objective of excellence
in research, scholarship, and education.

Oxford   New York
Auckland   Cape Town   Dar es Salaam   Hong Kong   Karachi
Kuala Lumpur   Madrid   Melbourne   Mexico City   Nairobi
New Delhi   Shanghai   Taipei   Toronto

With offices in
Argentina   Austria   Brazil   Chile   Czech Republic   France   Greece
Guatemala   Hungary   Italy   Japan   Poland   Portugal   Singapore
South Korea   Switzerland   Thailand   Turkey   Ukraine   Vietnam

Copyright © 2007 by Tickle, Incorporated

Published by Oxford University Press, Inc.
198 Madison Avenue, New York, NY 10016
www.oup.com

Oxford is a registered trademark of Oxford University Press
The Divine Hours™ Tickle, Inc.

Library of Congress Cataloging-in-Publication Data
The divine hours / compiled and with
an introduction by Phyllis Tickle. — Pocket ed.
p. cm.
ISBN 978-0-19-531693-3
1. Divine office—Texts.
I. Tickle, Phyllis.
BV 199.D3D58 2007
264'.15—dc22
2006036250

16
Printed in the United States of America
on acid-free paper

Contents

An Introduction
to This Manual

Christians who keep the hours as part of their spiritual practice often desire the convenience of an easily transported set of offices for occasions like traveling or business engagements when a complete manual is both cumbersome and awkward. This book is a direct result of that perceived and frequently voiced need.

Fixed-hour prayer, often known as observing the hours or keeping the offices, is one of the seven spiritual disciplines that came directly into Christianity from Judaism. Like tithing, observance of the Sabbath, fasting, or following the liturgical year, it informed the spiritual life of Our Lord and of the twelve Apostles, just as it informs and shapes the faith and practices of millions of Christians today.

Those already familiar with either *The Divine Hours*™, on which this pocket manual is based, or with any other of the many breviaries and fixed-hour prayerbooks available today will find their way easily through the use of these pages. Those for whom observing the divine hours is a new practice, may want an added word or two of instruction.

First, there are seven offices observed in each day . . . or there are seven provided. Most lay Christians find themselves unable to observe all seven and choose, instead, to select for observation those hours that are most compatible with their individual schedules and daily lives. It is important to remember, as pastors frequently remind us, that it is not the prayers we do not say but rather those we do say that matter to God.

The offices in this pocket manual are designed for individual or private use, but they can be readily converted to corporate use by changing singular pronouns in the appropriate places to plural ones. Likewise, the assumption here is that there will not be an officiant other than the pray-er. Should there be an officiant present, he or she should read the section titles or rubrics as well as lead the prayers.

A word or two of added observation might also be appropriate here. This is a pocket or travel edition. As such, it contains forty-nine offices, one for each divine hour of each day for one week. Given that structure, it can not reflect the nuances and rhythms of the liturgical year. In order to accommodate (in so far as is possible in an abbreviated volume) for this limitation, a chapter of "Traditional, Seasonal, and Occasional Prayers" has been included here as the final section of the book. When one is using the pocket edition on a holiday, for example, one may wish to add a Seasonal Prayer appropriate to that event, for example, an Advent prayer during Advent at the end of an office and just before the concluding prayer or blessing or petition. In the same manner, prayers from the Occasional Prayers may be added for those passing through life-changes like marriage or birth or illness; or prayers from the Traditional Prayers may be appropriate in moments of special petition or thanksgiving. It also should go without saying that no pocket edition is an entirely satisfactory substitute for a complete breviary or prayer manual, nor is it intended to be. A pocket edition can be a place to begin, or a companion on one's travels, or a tool readily at hand in one's purse or briefcase; but it should not long continue to be more than that.

Finally, a word about the symbols used in this book: The Office of Midnight is observed on the hour or half hour between 10:30 p.m. of the concluding day to 1:30 a.m. of the new day. Because it is sometimes very easy in the late hours of a concluding day simply to turn to that day and not to the offices for the approaching day, the *Pocket Edition* has a ✧ placed in the heading of the Office of Midnight to jog weary memories.

Additionally, for those who wish to chant or sing the offices, the psalms are pointed here, as in the larger manuals of *The Divine Hours*™, to show the breaks in the lines with an asterisk (*) as the symbol. In general, those singing the office will chant in a comfortable monotone, raising their voices by one full tone on the last accented syllable before the asterisk. The last accented syllable before the end of a line is lowered a full tone. Pronouns like "he," "she," "thee," "me" are never raised or lowered, this change falling on the immediately preceding accented syllable.

The only thing left to say, then, is that prayer is always a place as well as an action, and the daily offices are like small chapels or wayside stations within the day's courses. May grace attend all who enter there.

THE

DIVINE HOURS™

POCKET EDITION

SUNDAY

The Office of Midnight   To Be Observed on the Hour or Half Hour
Between 10:30 p.m. ✧ and 1:30 a.m.

The Call to Prayer
Praise the LORD, all you nations;* laud him, all you peoples.
For his loving-kindness toward us is great,* and the faithfulness of the LORD
    endures forever. Hallelujah!

Psalm 117

The Request for Presence
O LORD, let my prayer be set forth in your sight as incense,* the lifting up of my
    hands as the evening sacrifice.

Psalm 141:2, adapted

The Greeting
Our Father, forgive us our sins as we forgive those who have sinned against us.

The Canticle   *Song of Praise*
Benedictus es, Domine

Glory to you, Lord God of our fathers;*
    you are worthy of praise; glory to you.
Glory to you for the radiance of you holy Name;*
    we will praise you and highly exalt you for ever.
Glory to you in the splendor of your temple;*
    on the throne of your majesty, glory to you.
Glory to you, seated between the Cherubim;*
    we will praise you and highly exalt you for ever.
Glory to you, beholding the depths;*
    in the high vault of heaven, glory to you.
Glory to you, Father, Son, and Holy Spirit;*
    we will praise you and highly exalt you for ever.

Song of the Three Young Men, 29–34

The Psalm   *Serve the LORD with Gladness*
Be joyful in the LORD all you lands;* serve the LORD with gladness and come before
    his presence with a song.

Know this: The LORD himself is God;* he himself has made us, and we are his; we
  are his people and the sheep of his pasture.
Enter his gates with thanksgiving; go into his courts with praise;* give thanks to him
  and call upon his Name.
For the LORD is good; his mercy is everlasting;* and his faithfulness endures from
  age to age.

Psalm 100:1–4

The Gloria

The Small Verse

For David says concerning him, "I saw the Lord always before me, for he is at my
  right hand that I may not be shaken; therefore my heart was glad, and my tongue
  rejoiced; moreover my flesh will dwell in hope."

Acts 2:25–26

The Final Thanksgiving

I will greatly rejoice in the LORD, my soul shall exult in my God; for he has clothed
  me with the garments of salvation, he has covered me with the robe of
  righteousness, as a bridegroom decks himself with a garland, and as a bride
  adorns herself with her jewels.

Isaiah 61:10

The Petition

May the Lord GOD, father of all mercy, grant us who dwell here a peaceful night and
  a perfect end. *Amen.*

Office of the Night Watch   To Be Observed on the Hour or Half Hour
Between 1:30 and 4:30 a.m.

The Call to Prayer

Behold now, bless the LORD, all you servants of the LORD,* you that stand by night
  in the house of the LORD.

3

Lift up your hands in the holy place and bless the LORD;* the LORD who made
heaven and earth bless you out of Zion.

Psalm 134

The Request for Presence
O God, come to my assistance.
O Lord, make haste to help me.

The Greeting
I will offer you the sacrifice of thanksgiving* and call upon the Name of the LORD.

Psalm 116:15

The Refrain for the Night Watch
The heavens declare the glory of God,* and the firmament shows his handiwork.
One day tells its tale to another,* and one night imparts knowledge to another.

Psalm 19:1–2

The Psalm   You Brought Us Out into a Place of Refreshment
You brought us into the snare;* you laid heavy burdens upon our backs.
You let enemies ride over our heads; we went through fire and water;* but you
brought us out into a place of refreshment.
I will enter your house with burnt-offerings and will pay you my vows,* which I
promised with my lips and spoke with my mouth when I was in trouble.

Psalm 66:10–12

The Refrain
The heavens declare the glory of God,* and the firmament shows his handiwork.
One day tells its tale to another,* and one night imparts knowledge to another.

A Reading
The great saints and ancient prophets frequently experienced the alternation of up
and down, joy and sorrow. . . . If the great saints are exposed to such variations,
we who are poor and weak should not be discouraged if our spiritual life fails to
be uniformly ecstatic. The Holy Spirit gives and takes according to his own
divine purpose. I have never met anyone so religious and devout that he has not
felt occasionally some withdrawing of grace.

Thomas à Kempis (ca. 1421 CE) The Imitation of Christ

4

The Refrain

The heavens declare the glory of God,* and the firmament shows his handiwork.
One day tells its tale to another,* and one night imparts knowledge to another.

The Litany

For the peace from above, for the loving-kindness of God, and for the salvation of
my soul, I pray to the Lord.

Lord, have mercy.

For the peace of the world, for the welfare of the Holy Church of God, and for the
unity of all peoples, I pray to the Lord.

Lord, have mercy.

For the leaders of the nations and for all in authority, I pray to the Lord.

Lord, have mercy.

For the aged and infirm, for the widowed and orphans, and for the sick and the
suffering, I pray to the Lord.

Lord, have mercy.

For the poor and the oppressed, for the unemployed and the destitute, for prisoners
and captives, and for all who remember and care for them, I pray to the Lord.

Lord, have mercy.

For all who have died in the hope of the resurrection, and for all the departed, I pray
to the Lord.

Lord, have mercy.

The Thanksgiving

Lord, you now have set your servant free to go in peace as you have promised; for
these eyes of mine have seen the Savior whom you have prepared for all the
world to see: A Light to enlighten the nations, and the glory of your people
Israel. *Amen.*

Nunc Dimittis

The Final Petition

Now guide me waking, O Lord, and guard me sleeping; that awake I may watch with
Christ, and asleep, I may rest in peace. *Amen.*

The Office of Dawn **To Be Observed on the Hour or Half Hour**
Between 4:30 and 7:30 a.m.

The Call to Prayer
Hallelujah! How good it is to sing praises to our God!* how pleasant it is to honor
him with praise!

Psalm 147:1

The Request for Presence
My soul waits for the LORD, more than watchmen for the morning,* more than
watchmen for the morning.

Psalm 130:5

The Greeting
Glory be to the Father, and the Son, and the Holy Spirit.
As it was in the beginning, it is now
And ever shall be, world without end. *Amen.*

Gloria Patri

The Hymn
Immortal, invisible, God only wise,
in light inaccessible hid from our eyes,
most blessed, most glorious, the Ancient of Days,
almighty, victorious, your great name we praise.

Unresting, unhasting, and silent as light,
not wanting, not wasting, you rule us in might;
your justice like mountains high soaring above
your clouds which are fountains of goodness and love.

To all, our life you have given, both great and small;
in all life you are living, the true life of all;
we blossom and flourish as leaves on the tree,
and wither and perish, but naught changes thee.

Walter Chalmers Smith

6

The Psalm   *He Covers the Heavens with Clouds*

He covers the heavens with clouds* and prepares rain for the earth;

He makes grass to grow upon the mountains* and green plants to serve mankind.

He provides food for flocks and herds* and for the young ravens when they cry.

He is not impressed by the might of a horse;* he has no pleasure in the strength of
a man;

But the LORD has pleasure in those who fear him,* in those who await his gracious
favor.

Psalm 147:8–12

The Gloria in Excelsis

Glory to God in the highest, and on earth peace to people of good will.

We praise you.

We bless you.

We adore you.

We glorify you.

We give thanks to you for your great glory.

The Small Verse

Thus says the LORD: "Heaven is my throne and the earth is my footstool. . . . All
these things my hand has made, and so all these things are mine, says the LORD.
But this is the man to whom I will look, he that is humble and contrite in spirit
and trembles at my word."

Isaiah 66:1–2

The Lord's Prayer

The Final Blessing

May the Lord bless us and keep us and cause His face to shine upon us from this
day forth and forever more. *Amen.*

The Morning Office   **To Be Observed on the Hour or Half Hour
Between 6 and 9 a.m.**

The Call to Prayer

Love the Lord, all you who worship him;* the Lord protects the faithful, but repays
    to the full those who act haughtily.
Be strong and let your heart take courage,* all you who wait for the Lord.

Psalm 31:23–24

The Request for Presence

Hear, O Shepherd of Israel, leading Joseph like a flock;* shine forth, you that are
    enthroned upon the cherubim.

Psalm 80:1

The Greeting

How great is your goodness, O Lord!* which you have laid up for those who fear
    you; which you have done in the sight of all.

Psalm 31: 19

The Refrain for the Morning Lessons

I will bear witness that the Lord is righteous;* I will praise the name of the Lord
    Most High.

Psalm 7:18

A Reading

When the Pharisees saw this, they said to him, "Look, your disciples are doing what
    is forbidden on the sabbath." He answered, "Have you not read what David did
    when he and his men were hungry? He went into the house of God and ate
    the sacred bread, though neither he nor his men had a right to eat it, but only
    the priests. Or have you not read in the law that on the sabbath the priests in the
    temple break the sabbath and they are not held guilty? But I tell you, there is
    something greater than the temple here. If you had known what this text means,
    'It is mercy I require, not sacrifice,' you would not have condemned the innocent.
    For the Son of Man is lord of the sabbath."

Matthew 12:2–8

The Refrain

I will bear witness that the LORD is righteous;* I will praise the name of the LORD
Most High.

The Morning Psalm   *Praise the Name of the LORD*

Praise the LORD from the earth,* you sea-monsters and all deeps;
Fire and hail, snow and fog,* tempestuous wind, doing his will;
Mountains and all hills,* fruit trees and all cedars;
Wild beasts and all cattle,* creeping things and winged birds;
Kings of the earth and all peoples,* princes and all rulers of the world;
Young men and maidens,* old and young together.
Let them praise the Name of the LORD,*

Psalm 148:7–13a

The Refrain

I will bear witness that the LORD is righteous;* I will praise the name of the LORD
Most High.

The Gloria

The Lord's Prayer

The Prayer Appointed for the Day

Lord God, whose Son our Savior Jesus Christ, triumphed over the powers of death
and prepared for us our place in the new Jerusalem: Grant that I, who have this
day given thanks for his resurrection, may praise you in the City of which he is
the light, and where he lives and reigns for ever and ever. *Amen.*

The Concluding Prayer of the Church

Lord God, almighty and everlasting Father, you have brought me in safety to the
beginning of this day: Preserve me with your mighty power, that I may not fall
into sin, nor be overcome by adversity; and in all I do, direct me to the fulfilling
of your purposes; through Jesus Christ my Lord. *Amen.*

9

The Midday Office   **To Be Observed on the Hour or Half Hour**
Between 11 a.m. and 2 p.m.

The Call to Prayer
Let Israel rejoice in his Maker;* let the children of Zion be joyful in their King.

Psalm 149:2

The Request for Presence
May God be merciful to us and bless us,* show us the light of his countenance and
come to us.

Psalm 67:1

The Greeting
You are to be praised, O God, in Zion. . . . To you that hear prayer shall all flesh
come,* because of their transgressions.

Psalm 65:1–2

The Refrain for the Midday Lessons
I will confess you among the peoples, O LORD;* I will sing praises to you among the
nations.

Psalm 108:3

A Reading
With all this in mind, what are we to say? If God is on our side, who is against us?
He did not spare his own Son, but gave him up for us all; how can he fail to lavish
every gift upon us? Who will bring a charge against those whom God has chosen?
Not God, who acquits! Not Christ, who died, or rather rose again; not Christ who
is at God's right hand and pleads our cause! Then what can separate us from the
love of Christ? . . . For I am convinced that there is nothing in death or life, in the
realm of the spirits or superhuman powers, in the world as it is or in the world as
it shall be, in the forces of the universe, in heights or depths—nothing in all
creation that can separate us from the love of God in Christ Jesus our Lord.

Romans 8:31–39

The Refrain
I will confess you among the peoples, O LORD;* I will sing praises to you among the
nations

The Midday Psalm   *In God I Trust and Will Not Be Afraid*

In God the LORD, whose word I praise, in God I trust and will not be afraid,* for
    what can *mortals do to me?*

I am bound by the vow I made to you, O God;* I will present to you thank-offerings;

For you have rescued my soul from death and my feet from stumbling,* that I may
    walk before God in the light of the living.

Psalm 56:10–12

The Refrain

I will confess you among the peoples, O LORD;* I will sing praises to you among the
    nations

The Gloria

The Lord's Prayer

The Prayer Appointed for the Day

Lord God, whose Son our Savior Jesus Christ, triumphed over the powers of death
    and prepared for us our place in the new Jerusalem: Grant that I, who have this
    day given thanks for his resurrection, may praise you in the City of which he is
    the light, and where he lives and reigns for ever and ever. *Amen.*

The Concluding Prayer of the Church

O Lord my God, to you and to your service I devote myself, body, soul, and spirit. Fill
    my memory with the record of your mighty works; enlighten my understanding
    with the light of your Holy Spirit; and may all the desires of my heart and will
    center in what you would have me do. Make me an instrument of your salvation for
    the people entrusted to my care, and let me by my life and speaking set forth your
    true and living Word. Be always with me in carrying out the duties of my salvation;
    in praises heighten my love and gratitude; in speaking of You give me readiness of
    thought and expression; and grant that, by the clearness and brightness of your
    holy Word, all the world may be drawn to your blessed kingdom. All this I ask for
    the sake of your Son, my Savior Jesus Christ. *Amen.*

The Vespers Office   **To Be Observed on the Hour or Half Hour**
Between 5 and 8 p.m.

The Call to Prayer

Come now and see the works of God,* how wonderful he is in his doing toward all
people.

Psalm 66:4

The Request for Presence

Hear my cry, O God,* and listen to my prayer.

Psalm 61:1

The Greeting

I will dwell in your house for ever;*
For you, O God, have heard my vows;* you have granted me the heritage of those
who fear your Name.

Psalm 61:4a–5

The Hymn

There is a place of quiet rest,
Near to the heart of God;
A place where sin cannot molest,
Near to the heart of God.
O Jesus, blest Redeemer,
Sent from the heart of God,
Hold us who wait before you
Near to the heart of God.

There is a place of full release,
Near to the heart of God;
A place where all is joy and peace,
Near to the heart of God.
O Jesus, blessed redeemer,
Sent from the heart of God,
Hold us who wait before you
Near to the heart of God.

There is a place of comfort sweet,
Near to the heart of God;
A place where we and the Savior meet,
Near to the heart of God.
O Jesus, blessed Redeemer,
Sent from the heart of God,
Hold us who wait before you
Near to the heart of God.

Cleland McAfee

The Refrain for the Vespers Lessons

Behold, God is my helper;* it is the Lord who sustains my life.

Psalm 54:4

The Vespers Psalm   *You, O LORD, Are My Lamp*

With the faithful you show yourself faithful, O God;* with the forthright you show
   yourself forthright.
With the pure you show yourself pure,* but with the crooked you are wily.
You will save a lowly people,* but you will humble the haughty eyes.
You, O LORD, are my lamp;* my God, you make my darkness bright.

Psalm 18:26–29

The Refrain

Behold, God is my helper;* it is the Lord who sustains my life.

The Gloria

The Lord's Prayer

The Prayer Appointed for the Day

Lord God, whose Son our Savior Jesus Christ, triumphed over the powers of death
   and prepared for us our place in the new Jerusalem: Grant that I, who have this
   day given thanks for his resurrection, may praise you in the City of which he is
   the light, and where he lives and reigns for ever and ever. *Amen.*

The Concluding Prayer of the Church

Almighty and everlasting God, by whose Spirit the whole body of your faithful is
   governed and sanctified: Receive my supplications and prayers which I offer

13

before you for all members of your holy Church, that in our vocation and ministry in the week to come we all may truly serve you through our Lord and Savior Jesus Christ. *Amen.*

The Office of Compline   To Be Observed Before Retiring

The Call to Prayer
May the Lord Almighty grant me and those I love a peaceful night and a perfect end. *Amen.*

The Request for Presence
Our help is in the Name of the Lord; the maker of heaven and earth.

The Greeting
Almighty God, my heavenly Father, I have sinned against you, through my own fault in thought, and word, and deed, in what I have done and what I have left undone. For the sake of your Son our Lord Jesus Christ, forgive me all my offenses; and grant that I may serve you in newness of life, to the glory of your Name. *Amen.*

The Reading
How beautiful on the mountains are the feet of the herald,
the bringer of good news,
announcing deliverance,
proclaiming to Zion, "Your God has become king."
Your watchmen raise their voices and shout together in joy;
for with their own eyes they see
the LORD return to Zion.
Break forth together into shouts of joy,
you ruins of Jerusalem;
for the LORD has comforted his people,
he has redeemed Jerusalem.

The LORD has bared his holy arm
in the sight of all nations,
and the whole world from end to end
shall see the deliverance wrought by our God.

Isaiah 52:7–10

The Gloria

The Psalm   *The LORD Takes Pleasure in His People*

Let Israel rejoice in his Maker;* let the children of Zion be joyful in their King.
Let them praise his Name in the dance;* let them sing praise to him with timbrel
    and harp.
For the LORD takes pleasure in his people* and adorns the poor with victory.
Let the faithful rejoice in triumph;* let them be joyful on their beds.

Psalm 149:2–5

The Gloria

The Small Verse

Into your hands, O Lord, I commend my spirit; For you have redeemed me, O Lord,
    O God of truth. Keep me, O Lord, as the apple of your eye; Hide me under the
    shadow of your wings.

The Lord's Prayer

The Petition

Keep watch, dear Lord, with those who work, or watch, or weep this night, and give
    your angels charge over those who sleep. Tend the sick, Lord Christ; give rest to
    the weary, bless the dying, soothe the suffering, pity the afflicted, shield the
    joyous; and all for your love's sake. *Amen.*

The Final Thanksgiving

Lord, you now have set your servant free to go in peace as you have promised; for
    these eyes of mine have seen the Savior, whom you have prepared for all the
    world to see: a Light to enlighten the nations, and the glory of your people Israel.
    Glory to the Father, and to the Son, and to the Holy Spirit: as it was in the
    beginning, is now, and ever more shall be. *Amen.*

MONDAY

The Office of Midnight　　　**To Be Observed on the Hour or Half Hour**
Between 10:30 p.m.✧ and 1:30 a.m.

The Call to Prayer

Let all who seek you rejoice and be glad in you;* let those who love your salvation
　　say for ever, "Great is the LORD!"

Psalm 70:4

The Request for Presence

O LORD, let my prayer be set forth in your sight as incense,* the lifting up of my
　　hands as the evening sacrifice.

Psalm 141:2, adapted

The Greeting

Our Father, give us this day our daily bread.

The Canticle　　　　　　　　　　　　　　*The First Song of Isaiah*
Ecce, Deus

Surely, it is God who saves me;*
　　I will trust in him and not be afraid.
For the Lord is my stronghold and my sure defense,*
　　and he will be my Savior.
Therefore you shall draw water with rejoicing*
　　from the springs of salvation.
And on that day you shall say,*
　　Give thanks to the Lord and call upon his Name;
Make his deeds known among the peoples;*
　　see that they remember that his Name is exalted.
Sing praises of the Lord, for he has done great things,*
　　and this is known in all the world.
Cry aloud, inhabitants of Zion, ring out your joy,*
　　for the great one in the midst of you is the Holy One of Israel.

Isaiah 12:2–6

The Psalm　　　　　　　　　　　　　　　*Be My Strong Rock*

In you, O LORD, have I taken refuge;* let me never be ashamed.
Be my strong rock, a castle to keep me safe;* you are my crag and my stronghold.

For you are my hope, O Lord GOD,* my confidence since I was young.

I have been sustained by you ever since I was born; from my mother's womb you
have been my strength;* my praise shall be always of you.

Let my mouth be full of your praise* and your glory all the day long.

Psalm 71:1ff

The Gloria

The Small Verse

Therefore, if any one is in Christ, he is a new creation; the old has passed away,
behold, the new has come. All this is from God, who through Christ reconciled
us to himself.

2 Corinthians 5:17–18a

The Final Thanksgiving

I will greatly rejoice in the LORD, my soul shall exult in my God; for he has clothed
me with the garments of salvation, he has covered me with the robe of righteousness, as a bridegroom decks himself with a garland, and as a bride adorns
herself with her jewels.

Isaiah 61:10

The Petition

May the Lord GOD, father of grace and mercy, grant all who dwell here a peaceful
night and a perfect end. *Amen.*

꒳

Office of the Night Watch   To Be Observed on the Hour or Half Hour
Between 1:30 and 4:30 a.m.

The Call to Prayer

Behold now, bless the LORD, all you servants of the LORD,* you that stand by night
in the house of the LORD.

Lift up your hands in the holy place and bless the LORD;* the LORD who made
heaven and earth bless you out of Zion.

Psalm 134

The Request for Presence

O God, come to my assistance.
O Lord, make haste to help me.

The Greeting

Out of Zion, perfect in its beauty,* God reveals himself in glory.

Psalm 50:2

The Refrain for the Night Watch

It is a good thing to give thanks to the LORD,* and to sing praises to your Name,
   O Most High;
To tell of your loving-kindness early in the morning* and of your faithfulness in the
   night season.

Psalm 92:1–2

The Psalm   Praise the LORD

Hallelujah! Praise the Name of the LORD;* give praise, you servants of the LORD,
You who stand in the house of the LORD,* in the courts of the house of our God.
Praise the LORD, for the LORD is good;* sing praises to his Name, for it is lovely.

Psalm 135:1–3

The Refrain

It is a good thing to give thanks to the LORD,* and to sing praises to your Name,
   O Most High;
To tell of your loving-kindness early in the morning* and of your faithfulness in the
   night season.

A Reading

Man is placed above all creatures, and not beneath them, and he cannot be satisfied
   or content except in something greater than himself. Greater than himself there
   is nothing but Myself, the Eternal God. Therefore, it is the "I" alone that can
   satisfy us.

St. Catherine of Siena (1347–80 CE), The Dialogue

The Refrain

It is a good thing to give thanks to the LORD,* and to sing praises to your Name,
   O Most High;

To tell of your loving-kindness early in the morning* and of your faithfulness in the night season.

The Litany

Father, I pray for your holy catholic Church;
> *That we all may be one.*

Grant that every member of the Church may truly and humbly serve you;
> *That your Name may be glorified by all people.*

I pray for all who govern and hold authority in the nations of the world;
> *That there may be justice and peace on the earth.*

Have compassion on those who suffer from any grief or trouble;
> *That they may be delivered from their distress.*

Give to the departed eternal rest.
> *Let light perpetual shine upon them.*

I praise you for your saints who have entered into joy;
> *May I also come to share in your heavenly kingdom.*

The Thanksgiving

Lord, you now have set your servant free to go in peace as you have promised; for these eyes of mine have seen the Savior whom you have prepared for all the world to see: A Light to enlighten the nations, and the glory of your people Israel. *Amen.*

Nunc Dimittis

The Final Petition

Now guide me waking, O Lord, and guard me sleeping; that awake I may watch with Christ, and asleep, I may rest in peace. *Amen.*

The Office of Dawn   **To Be Observed on the Hour or Half Hour**
Between 4:30 and 7:30 a.m.

The Call to Prayer

Hallelujah! Praise the LORD, O my soul!* I will praise the LORD, as long as I live; I
will sing praises to my God while I have my being.

Psalm 146:1

The Request for Presence

My soul waits for the LORD, more than watchmen for the morning,* more than
watchmen for the morning.

Psalm 130:5

The Greeting

Glory be to the Father, and the Son, and the Holy Spirit.
As it was in the beginning, it is now
And ever shall be, world without end. *Amen.*

Gloria Patri

The Hymn

Love divine, all loves excelling,
joy of heaven, to earth come down;
fix in us your humble dwelling;
all your faithful mercies crown!
Jesus, thou art all compassion,
pure, unbounded love thou art;
visit us with your salvation;
enter every trembling heart.

Come, Almighty to deliver,
let us all your life receive;
suddenly return and never,
nevermore your temples leave.
You we would be always blessing,
serve you as your hosts above,

pray and praise you without ceasing,
glory in your perfect love.

Charles Wesley

The Psalm   *Praise the Name of the LORD*

Praise the LORD, from the heavens;* praise him in the heights.

Praise him, all you angels of his;* praise him, all his host.

Praise him, sun and moon;* praise him, all you shining stars.

Praise him, heaven of heavens,* and you waters above the heavens.

Let them praise the Name of the LORD;* for he commanded, and they were created.

He made them stand fast for ever and ever;* he gave them a law which shall not
pass away.

Psalm 148:1b–6

The Gloria in Excelsis

Glory to God in the highest, and on earth peace to people of good will.

We praise you.

We bless you.

We adore you.

We glorify you.

We give thanks to you for your great glory.

The Small Verse

A voice cries: "In the wilderness prepare the way of the LORD, Make straight in the
desert a highway for our God. Every valley shall be lifted up, and every
mountain and hill be made low; the uneven ground shall become level, and the
rough places a plain. And the glory of the Lord, shall be revealed, and all flesh
shall see it together, for the mouth of the Lord has spoken."

Isaiah 40:3–5

The Lord's Prayer

The Final Blessing

May the Lord bless us and keep us and cause His face to shine upon us from this
day forth and forever more. *Amen.*

෨

The Morning Office   **To Be Observed on the Hour or Half Hour**
Between 6 and 9 a.m.

The Call to Prayer
Let everything that has breath* praise the LORD. Hallelujah!

Psalm 150:6

The Request for Presence
Incline your ear to me;* make haste to deliver me.

Psalm 31:2

The Greeting
Glory be to the Father, and the Son, and the Holy Spirit.
As it was in the beginning, it is now
And ever shall be, world without end. *Amen.*

Gloria Patri

The Refrain for the Morning Lessons
You strengthen me more and more;* you enfold and comfort me.

Psalm 71:21

A Reading
Jesus said: 'The Father loves the Son and has entrusted him with complete authority.
    Whoever puts his faith in the Son has eternal life. Whoever disobeys the Son will
    not see life; God's wrath rests upon him.'

John 3:35–36

The Refrain
You strengthen me more and more;* you enfold and comfort me.

The Morning Psalm   *He Covers the Heavens with Clouds*
He covers the heavens with clouds* and prepares rain for the earth;
He makes grass to grow upon the mountains* and green plants to serve mankind.
He provides food for flocks and herds* and for the young ravens when they cry.
He is not impressed by the might of a horse;* he has no pleasure in the strength
    of a man;

But the LORD has pleasure in those who fear him,* in those who await his gracious favor.

Psalm 147:8–12

The Refrain

You strengthen me more and more;* you enfold and comfort me.

The Gloria

The Lord's Prayer

The Prayer Appointed for the Day

O Lord, you have taught us that without love, whatever we do is worth nothing: Send your Holy Spirit and pour into my heart your greatest gift, which is love, the true bond of peace and of all virtue, without which whoever lives is accounted dead before you. Grant this for the sake of your only Son Jesus Christ, who lives and reigns with you and the Holy Spirit, one God, now and for ever. *Amen.*

The Concluding Prayer of the Church

Lord God, almighty and everlasting Father, you have brought me in safety to the beginning of this day: Preserve me with your mighty power, that I may not fall into sin, nor be overcome by adversity; and in all I do, direct me to the fulfilling of your purposes; through Jesus Christ my Lord. *Amen.*

꒒

The Midday Office

To Be Observed on the Hour or Half Hour Between 11 a.m. and 2 p.m.

The Call to Prayer

Hallelujah! Sing to the LORD a new song;* sing his praise in the congregation of the faithful.

Psalm 149:1

The Request for Presence
O God, come to my assistance.
O Lord, make haste to help me.

The Greeting
I give you thanks, O God, I give you thanks,* calling upon your Name and declaring
all your wonderful deeds.

Based on Psalm 75:1

The Refrain for the Midday Lessons
Your love, O LORD, for ever will I sing;* from age to age my mouth will proclaim
your faithfulness.

Psalm 89:1

A Reading
Faith gives substance to our hopes and convinces us of realities we do not see.

Hebrews 11:1

The Refrain
Your love, O LORD, for ever will I sing;* from age to age my mouth will proclaim
your faithfulness.

The Psalm   *Praise the LORD from the Earth*
Praise the LORD from the earth,* you sea-monsters and all deeps;
Fire and hail, snow and fog,* tempestuous wind, doing his will;
Mountains and all hills,* fruit trees and all cedars;
Wild beasts and all cattle,* creeping things and winged birds;
Kings of the earth and all peoples,* princes and all rulers of the world;
Young men and maidens,* old and young together.
Let them praise the Name of the LORD,*

Psalm 148:7–13a

The Refrain
Your love, O LORD, for ever will I sing;* from age to age my mouth will proclaim
your faithfulness.

The Gloria

The Lord's Prayer

The Prayer Appointed for the Day

O Lord, you have taught us that without love, whatever we do is worth nothing:
Send your Holy Spirit and pour into my heart your greatest gift, which is love,
the true bond of peace and of all virtue, without which whoever lives is
accounted dead before you. Grant this for the sake of your only Son Jesus Christ,
who lives and reigns with you and the Holy Spirit, one God, now and for ever.
Amen.

The Concluding Prayer of the Church

Let us bless the Lord God living and true! Let us always render him praise, glory,
honor, blessing, and all good things! Amen. Amen. So be it! So be it!

St. Francis of Assisi

ↄ

The Vespers Office   **To Be Observed on the Hour or Half Hour
Between 5 and 8 p.m.**

The Call to Prayer

Bless God in the congregation;* bless the LORD, you that are of the fountain of
Israel.

Psalm 68:26

The Request for Presence

O LORD, let my prayer be set forth in your sight as incense,* the lifting up of my
hands as the evening sacrifice.

Psalm 141:2, adapted

The Greeting

Father, Yours are the kingdom, the power, and the glory forever.

The Hymn

The love we give each other
Is that which builds us up.
We live in one another;
We share a common cup.
Our loves are each a whisper
Of one sweet voice divine,
And when we sing together
The chorus is sublime.

Glory to the Father
To the Son,
And to the Holy Spirit,
Blessed Three in One.
As in the beginning,
So it is now,
And evermore shall be.

Haskell Miller

The Refrain for the Vespers Lessons

The Lord is my shepherd and nothing is wanting to me. In green pastures He hath
    settled me.

Psalm 23:1

The Vespers Psalm   How Manifold Are Your Works

Bless the LORD, O my soul;* O LORD my God, how excellent is your greatness! you
    are clothed with majesty and splendor.
You wrap yourself with light as with a cloak* and spread out the heavens like a
    curtain.
You lay the beams of your chambers in the waters above;* you make the clouds your
    chariot; you ride on the wings of the wind.
You make the winds your messengers* and flames of fire your servants.
You have set the earth upon its foundations,* so that it never shall move at any time.
You covered it with the Deep as with a mantle;* the waters stood higher than the
    mountains.
At your rebuke they fled;* at the voice of your thunder they hastened away.

They went up into the hills and down to the valleys beneath,* to the places you had
  appointed for them.
O LORD, how manifold are your works!* in wisdom you have made them all; the
  earth is full of your creatures.

Psalm 104:1–8, 25

The Refrain

The Lord is my shepherd and nothing is wanting to me. In green pastures He hath
  settled me.

The Gloria

The Lord's Prayer

The Prayer Appointed for the Day

O Lord, you have taught us that without love, whatever we do is worth nothing:
  Send your Holy Spirit and pour into my heart your greatest gift, which is love,
  the true bond of peace and of all virtue, without which whoever lives is
  accounted dead before you. Grant this for the sake of your only Son Jesus Christ,
  who lives and reigns with you and the Holy Spirit, one God, now and for ever.
  Amen.

The Concluding Prayer of the Church

Protect us, Lord, as we stay awake; watch over us as we sleep, that awake we may
  watch with Christ, and asleep, rest in peace. *Amen.*

The Office of Compline   To Be Observed Before Retiring

The Call to Prayer

May the Lord Almighty grant me and those I love a peaceful night and a perfect end.
  Amen.

The Request for Presence

Our help is in the Name of the Lord; the maker of heaven and earth.

29

The Greeting

Almighty God, my heavenly Father, I have sinned against you, through my own
fault in thought, and word, and deed, in what I have done and what I have left
undone. For the sake of your Son our Lord Jesus Christ, forgive me all my
offenses; and grant that I may serve you in newness of life, to the glory of your
Name. *Amen.*

The Reading

O gracious Light,
pure brightness of the everlasting Father in heaven,
O Jesus Christ, holy and blessed!

Now as we come to the setting of the sun,
and our eyes behold the vesper light,
we sing your praises, O God: Father, Son, and Holy Spirit.

You are worthy at all times to be praised by happy voices,
O Son of God, O Giver of life,
and to be glorified through all the worlds.

Phos Hilaron

The Gloria

The Psalm   *How Manifold Are Your Works*

Bless the LORD, O my soul;* O LORD my God, how excellent is your greatness! you
are clothed with majesty and splendor.

You wrap yourself with light as with a cloak* and spread out the heavens like a
curtain.

You lay the beams of your chambers in the waters above;* you make the clouds your
chariot; you ride on the wings of the wind.

You make the winds your messengers* and flames of fire your servants.

You have set the earth upon its foundations,* so that it never shall move at any time.

You covered it with the Deep as with a mantle;* the waters stood higher than the
mountains.

At your rebuke they fled;* at the voice of your thunder they hastened away.

They went up into the hills and down to the valleys beneath,* to the places you had appointed for them.

O LORD, how manifold are your works!* in wisdom you have made them all; the earth is full of your creatures.

Psalm 104:1–8, 25

The Gloria

The Small Verse

Into your hands, O Lord, I commend my spirit; For you have redeemed me, O Lord, O God of truth. Keep me, O Lord, as the apple of your eye; Hide me under the shadow of your wings.

The Lord's Prayer

The Petition

Keep watch, dear Lord, with those who work, or watch, or weep this night, and give your angels charge over those who sleep. Tend the sick, Lord Christ; give rest to the weary, bless the dying, soothe the suffering, pity the afflicted, shield the joyous; and all for your love's sake. *Amen.*

The Final Thanksgiving

Lord, you now have set your servant free to go in peace as you have promised; for these eyes of mine have seen the Savior, whom you have prepared for all the world to see: a Light to enlighten the nations, and the glory of your people Israel. Glory to the Father, and to the Son, and to the Holy Spirit: as it was in the beginning, is now, and ever more shall be. *Amen.*

TUESDAY

The Office of Midnight   **To Be Observed on the Hour or Half Hour**
Between 10:30 p.m.✧ and 1:30 a.m.

The Call to Prayer
Search for the LORD and his strength;* continually seek his face.

Psalm 105:4

The Request for Presence
O LORD, let my prayer be set forth in your sight as incense,* the lifting up of my
hands as the evening sacrifice.

Psalm 141:2, adapted

The Greeting
Our Father, may Your kingdom come on earth as in Heaven.

The Canticle   *A Song of Creation–Part Two*
Benedicite, omnia opera Domini

Glorify the Lord, all you works of the Lord,*
  praise him and highly exalt him for ever.
In the firmament of his power, glorify the Lord,*
  praise him and highly exalt him for ever.
Let the earth glorify the Lord,*
  praise him and highly exalt him for ever.
Glorify the Lord, O mountains and hills, and all that grows upon the earth,*
  praise him and highly exalt him for ever.
Glorify the Lord, O springs of water, seas, and streams,*
  O whales and all that move in the waters.
All birds of the air, glorify the Lord,*
  praise him and highly exalt him for ever.
Glorify the Lord, O beasts of the wild,*
  and all you flocks and herds.
O men and women everywhere, glorify the Lord,*
  praise him and highly exalt him for ever.

Song of the Three Young Men, 52–61

The Psalm   ***O LORD, You Are My Portion and My Cup***

Protect me, O God, for I take refuge in you;* I have said to the LORD, "You are my
Lord, my good above all other."

All my delight is upon the godly that are in the land,* upon those who are noble
among the people.

But those who run after other gods* shall have their troubles multiplied.

Their libations of blood I will not offer,* nor take the names of their gods upon my
lips.

O LORD, you are my portion and my cup;* it is you who uphold my lot.

Psalm 16:1–5

The Gloria

The Small Verse

When the perishable puts on the imperishable, and the mortal puts on immortality,
then shall come to pass the saying that is written: "Death is swallowed up in
victory." "O death, where is thy victory? O death, where is thy sting?"

1 Corinthians 15:54–55

The Final Thanksgiving

I will greatly rejoice in the LORD, my soul shall exult in my God; for he has clothed
me with the garments of salvation, he has covered me with the robe of righteousness, as a bridegroom decks himself with a garland, and as a bride adorns
herself with her jewels.

Isaiah 61:10

The Petition

May the Lord GOD, father of all mercy, grant us who dwell here a peaceful night and
a perfect end. *Amen.*

Office of the Night Watch   To Be Observed on the Hour or Half Hour
Between 1:30 and 4:30 a.m.

The Call to Prayer

Behold now, bless the LORD, all you servants of the LORD,* you that stand by night
in the house of the LORD.

Lift up your hands in the holy place and bless the LORD;* the LORD who made
heaven and earth bless you out of Zion.

Psalm 134

The Request for Presence

O God, come to my assistance.
O Lord, make haste to help me.

The Greeting

You are to be praised, O God, in Zion. . . . To you that hear prayer shall all flesh
come,* because of their transgressions.

Psalm 65:1–2

The Refrain for the Night Watch

Happy are they who have not walked in the counsel of the wicked,* nor lingered in
the way of sinners, nor sat in the seats of the scornful!

Their delight is in the law of the LORD,* and they meditate on his law day and night.

Psalm 1:1–2

The Psalm   *You Are the LORD*

In sacrifice and offering you take no pleasure* (you have given me ears to hear you);
Burnt-offering and sin-offering you have not required,* and so I said, "Behold, I
come.

In the roll of the book it is written concerning me:* 'I love to do your will, O my
God; your law is deep in my heart.'"

I proclaimed righteousness in the great congregation;* behold, I did not restrain my
lips; and that, O LORD, you know.

Your righteousness have I not hidden in my heart; I have spoken of your faithfulness
and your deliverance;* I have not concealed your love and faithfulness from the
great congregation.

36

You are the LORD; do not withhold your compassion from me;* let your love and
   your faithfulness keep me safe for ever,

Psalm 40:7–12

The Refrain

Happy are they who have not walked in the counsel of the wicked,* nor lingered in
   the way of sinners, nor sat in the seats of the scornful!
Their delight is in the law of the LORD,* and they meditate on his law day and night.

A Reading

The law, if you use it aright, sends you to Christ. For since the law's aim is to justify
   humanity, and since it fails to effect this, it remits us to Him who can do so.
   Another way, again, of using the law lawfully is when we keep it, but as a thing
   superfluous. And how is a thing superfluous? As the bridle is properly used, not
   by the prancing horse that chomps it, but by the horse that wears it only for the
   sake of appearance; so he uses the law lawfully who governs himself, though not
   as constrained by the letter of it.

St. John Chrysostom, Bishop of Constantinople (ca. 347–407 CE),
Homily on the Epistle of St. Paul to Timothy

The Refrain

Happy are they who have not walked in the counsel of the wicked,* nor lingered in
   the way of sinners, nor sat in the seats of the scornful!
Their delight is in the law of the LORD,* and they meditate on his law day and night.

The Litany

O God the Father, Creator of heaven and earth,
   Have mercy upon me.
O God the Son, Redeemer of the world,
   Have mercy upon me.
O God the Holy Spirit, Sanctifier of the faithful,
   Have mercy upon me.
O holy, blessed, and glorious Trinity, one God,
   Have mercy upon me.
Remember not, Lord Christ, my offenses, nor the offenses of my forefathers; neither
   reward me according to my sins. Spare me, good Lord, spare your people, whom

you have redeemed with your most precious blood, and by your mercy preserve us, for ever.

Spare us, good Lord.

The Thanksgiving

Lord, you now have set your servant free to go in peace as you have promised; for these eyes of mine have seen the Savior whom you have prepared for all the world to see: A Light to enlighten the nations, and the glory of your people Israel. *Amen.*

Nunc Dimittis

The Final Petition

Now guide me waking, O Lord, and guard me sleeping; that awake I may watch with Christ, and asleep, I may rest in peace. *Amen.*

ॐ

The Office of Dawn   To Be Observed on the Hour or Half Hour
Between 4:30 and 7:30 a.m.

The Call to Prayer

Sing to the LORD with thanksgiving;* make music to our God upon the harp.

Psalm 147:7

The Request for Presence

My soul waits for the LORD, more than watchmen for the morning,* more than watchmen for the morning.

Psalm 130:5

The Greeting

Glory be to the Father, and the Son, and the Holy Spirit.
As it was in the beginning, it is now
And ever shall be, world without end. *Amen.*

Gloria Patri

38

The Hymn

My faith looks up to thee,
thou Lamb of Calvary,
    Savior divine!
Now hear me while I pray,
take all my guilt away,
O let me from this day
    be wholly thine!

May thy rich grace impart
strength to my fainting heart,
    my zeal inspire!
As thou hast died for me,
O may my love to thee
pure, warm, and changeless be,
    a living fire!

Ray Palmer

The Psalm   The LORD Adorns the Poor with Victory

Let Israel rejoice in his Maker;* let the children of Zion be joyful in their King.
Let them praise his Name in the dance;* let them sing praise to him with timbrel
    and harp.
For the LORD takes pleasure in his people* and adorns the poor with victory.
Let the faithful rejoice in triumph;* let them be joyful on their beds.

Psalm 149:2–5

The Gloria in Excelsis

Glory to God in the highest, and on earth peace to people of good will.
    We praise you.
    We bless you.
    We adore you.
    We glorify you.
We give thanks to you for your great glory.

The Small Verse

But he said to them, "You are those who justify yourselves before men, but God
knows your hearts; for what is exalted among men is an abomination in the sight
of God."

Luke 16:15

The Lord's Prayer

The Final Blessing

May the LORD bless us and keep us and cause His face to shine upon us from this
day forth and forever more. *Amen.*

ॐ

The Morning Office To Be Observed on the Hour or Half Hour Between 6 and 9 a.m.

The Call to Prayer

Let all the earth fear the LORD;* let all who dwell in the world stand in awe of him.

Psalm 33:8

The Request for Presence

Be my strong rock, a castle to keep me safe, for you are my crag and my stronghold.

Psalm 31:3a

The Greeting

My God, my rock in whom I put my trust,* my shield, the horn of my salvation, and
my refuge; you are worthy of praise.

Psalm 18:2

The Refrain for the Morning Lessons

Be strong and let your heart take courage,* all you who wait for the LORD.

Psalm 31:24

A Reading

Jesus said, Have no fear, little flock; for your Father has chosen to give you the
kingdom.

Luke 12:32

The Refrain

Be strong and let your heart take courage,* all you who wait for the LORD.

The Morning Psalm   *We Will Bless the LORD*

May you be blessed by the LORD,* the maker of heaven and earth.
The heaven of heavens is the LORD's,* but he entrusted the earth to its peoples.
The dead do not praise the LORD,* nor all those who go down into silence;
But we will bless the LORD,* from this time forth for evermore. Hallelujah!

Psalm 115:15–18

The Refrain

Be strong and let your heart take courage,* all you who wait for the LORD.

The Gloria

The Lord's Prayer

The Prayer Appointed for the Day

Grant me, Lord, not to be anxious about earthly things, but to love things heavenly;
and even now, while I am placed among things that are passing away, to hold fast
to those that shall endure; through Jesus Christ our Lord, who lives and reigns
with you and the Holy Spirit, one God, for ever and ever. *Amen.*

The Concluding Prayer of the Church

Lord God, almighty and everlasting Father, you have brought me in safety to the
beginning of this day: Preserve me with your mighty power, that I may not fall
into sin, nor be overcome by adversity; and in all I do, direct me to the fulfilling
of your purposes; through Jesus Christ my Lord. *Amen.*

The Midday Office   **To Be Observed on the Hour or Half Hour**
                                    Between 11 a.m. and 2 p.m.

The Call to Prayer

Blessed be the LORD, the God of Israel, from everlasting and to everlasting;* and let
   all people say, "Amen!" Hallelujah!

Psalm 106:48

The Request for Presence

O God, you are my God; eagerly I seek you;* my soul thirsts for you, my flesh faints
   for you, as in barren and dry land where there is no water.

Psalm 63:1

The Greeting

Your way, O God, is holy;* who is as great as our God?

Psalm 77:13

The Refrain for the Midday Lessons

Send forth your strength, O God;* establish, O God, what you have wrought for us.

Psalm 68:28

A Reading

Praise be to the God and Father of our Lord Jesus Christ, the all-merciful Father, the
   God whose consolation never fails us! He consoles us in all our troubles, so that
   we in turn may be able to console others in any trouble of theirs and to share
   with them the consolation we ourselves receive from God.

I Corinthians 1:3–4

The Refrain

Send forth your strength, O God;* establish, O God, what you have wrought for us.

The Midday Psalm   *The LORD Has Pleasure in Those who Fear Him*

He covers the heavens with clouds* and prepares rain for the earth;
He makes grass to grow upon the mountains* and green plants to serve mankind.
He provides food for flocks and herds* and for the young ravens when they cry.
He is not impressed by the might of a horse;* he has no pleasure in the strength
   of a man;

But the LORD has pleasure in those who fear him,* in those who await his gracious favor.

Psalm 147:8–12

The Refrain

Send forth your strength, O God;* establish, O God, what you have wrought for us.

The Gloria

The Lord's Prayer

The Prayer Appointed for the Day

Grant me, Lord, not to be anxious about earthly things, but to love things heavenly; and even now, while I am placed among things that are passing away, to hold fast to those that shall endure; through Jesus Christ our Lord, who lives and reigns with you and the Holy Spirit, one God, for ever and ever. *Amen.*

The Concluding Prayer of the Church

O God, who on the day of Pentecost taught the hearts of your faithful people by sending to them the light of your Holy Spirit: Grant me by that same Spirit to have a right judgment in all things, and evermore to rejoice in his holy comfort; through Jesus Christ your Son my Lord, who lives and reigns with you, in the unity of the Holy Spirit, one God, for ever and ever. *Amen.*

༈

The Vespers Office   **To Be Observed on the Hour or Half Hour Between 5 and 8 p.m.**

The Call to Prayer

Let the Name of the LORD be blessed,* from this time forth for evermore.
From the rising of the sun to its going down* let the Name of the LORD be praised.

Psalm 113:2–3

The Request for Presence

Give ear, O Lord, to my prayer.

Psalm 86:6

The Greeting
Blessed be the Lord God of Israel,* who alone does wondrous deeds!
And blessed be his glorious Name for ever!* And may all the earth be filled with
    his glory.
Amen. Amen.

Psalm 72:18–19

The Hymn
"Forgive our sins as we forgive,"
You taught us, Lord, to pray,
But you alone can grant us grace
To live the words we say

How can your pardon reach and bless
The unforgiving heart
That broods on wrongs and will not let
Old bitterness depart?

In blazing light your cross reveals
The truth we dimly knew:
What trivial debts are owed to us,
How great our debt to you!

Lord, cleanse the depths within our souls
And bid resentment cease.
Then, bound to all in bonds of love,
Our lives will spread your peace.

Rosamond E. Herklots

The Refrain for the Vespers Lessons
Bless the LORD, O my soul,* and forget not all his benefits.

Psalm 103:2

The Vespers Psalm   The Law of the LORD Is Perfect
The law of the LORD is perfect and revives the soul;* the testimony of the LORD is
    sure and gives wisdom to the innocent.

44

The statutes of the LORD are just and rejoice the heart;* the commandment of the
    LORD is clear and gives light to the eyes.
The fear of the LORD is clean and endures for ever;* the judgments of the LORD are
    true and righteous altogether.
More to be desired are they than gold, more than much fine gold,* sweeter far than
    honey, than honey in the comb.
By them also is your servant enlightened,* and in keeping them there is great reward.

Psalm 19:7–11

The Refrain
Bless the LORD, O my soul,* and forget not all his benefits.

The Gloria

The Lord's Prayer

The Prayer Appointed for the Day
Grant me, Lord, not to be anxious about earthly things, but to love things heavenly;
    and even now, while I am placed among things that are passing away, to hold fast
    to those that shall endure; through Jesus Christ our Lord, who lives and reigns
    with you and the Holy Spirit, one God, for ever and ever. *Amen.*

The Concluding Prayer of the Church
O God, you declare your almighty power chiefly in showing mercy and pity: Grant
    me the fullness of your grace, that I, running to obtain your promises, may
    become a partaker of your heavenly treasure; through Jesus Christ, our Lord, who
    lives and reigns with you and the Holy Spirit, one God, for ever and ever. *Amen.*

The Office of Compline   To Be Observed Before Retiring

The Call to Prayer
May the Lord Almighty grant me and those I love a peaceful night and a perfect end.
    Amen.

45

The Request for Presence

Our help is in the Name of the Lord; the maker of heaven and earth.

The Greeting

Almighty God, my heavenly Father, I have sinned against you, through my own fault in thought, and word, and deed, in what I have done and what I have left undone. For the sake of your Son our Lord Jesus Christ, forgive me all my offenses; and grant that I may serve you in newness of life, to the glory of your Name. *Amen.*

The Reading

Glory be to God for dappled things—
  For skies of couple-colour as a brinded cow;
  For rose-molds all in stipple upon trout that swim;
Fresh-firecoal chestnut-falls; finches' wings;
  Landscape plotted and pieced-fold, fallow, and plough;
  And all trades, their gear and tackle and trim.
All things counter, original, spare, strange;
  Whatever is fickle, freckled (who knows how?)
  With swift, slow, sweet, sour; adazzle, dim;
He fathers-forth whose beauty is past change:
  Praise him.

Gerald Manley Hopkins

The Gloria

The Psalm   **He Gives Snow Like Wool**

The LORD sends out his command to the earth,* and his word runs very swiftly.
He gives snow like wool;* he scatters hoarfrost like ashes.
He scatters his hail like bread crumbs;* who can stand against his cold?
He sends forth his word and melts them;* he blows with his wind, and the waters flow.

Psalm 147:13–19

The Gloria

The Small Verse

Into your hands, O Lord, I commend my spirit; For you have redeemed me, O Lord, O God of truth. Keep me, O Lord, as the apple of your eye; Hide me under the shadow of your wings.

The Lord's Prayer

The Petition

Keep watch, dear Lord, with those who work, or watch, or weep this night, and give your angels charge over those who sleep. Tend the sick, Lord Christ; give rest to the weary, bless the dying, soothe the suffering, pity the afflicted, shield the joyous; and all for your love's sake. *Amen.*

The Final Thanksgiving

Lord, you now have set your servant free to go in peace as you have promised; for these eyes of mine have seen the Savior, whom you have prepared for all the world to see: a Light to enlighten the nations, and the glory of your people Israel. Glory to the Father, and to the Son, and to the Holy Spirit: as it was in the beginning, is now, and ever more shall be. *Amen.*

WEDNESDAY

The Office of Midnight   **To Be Observed on the Hour or Half Hour**
                              Between 10:30 p.m. ✧ and 1:30 a.m.

The Call to Prayer

Sing to the LORD with the harp,* with the harp and the voice of song.
With trumpets and the sound of the horn* shout with joy before the King, the LORD.

Psalm 98:6–7

The Request for Presence

O LORD, let my prayer be set forth in your sight as incense,* the lifting up of my
    hands as the evening sacrifice.

Psalm 141:2, adapted

The Greeting

Our Father, forgive us our sins as we forgive those who have sinned against us.

The Canticle   *The Song of Mary*
Magnificat

My soul proclaims the greatness of the Lord, my spirit rejoices in God my Savior;*
    for he has looked with favor on his lowly servant.
From this day all generations will call me blessed:*
    the Almighty has done great things for me, and holy is his Name.
He has mercy on those who fear him*
    in every generation.
He has shown the strength of his arm,*
    he has scattered the proud in their conceit.
He has cast down the mighty from their thrones,*
    and has lifted up the lowly.
He has filled the hungry with good things,*
    and the rich he has sent away empty.
He has come to the help of his servant Israel,*
    for he has remembered his promise of mercy,
The promise he made to our fathers,*
    to Abraham and his children for ever.
Glory to the Father, and to the Son, and to the Holy Spirit:*
    as it was in the beginning, is now, and will be for ever. *Amen.*

Luke 1:46–55

The Psalm   ***The LORD Has Girded Himself with Strength***

The LORD is King; he has put on splendid apparel;* the LORD has put on his apparel
and girded himself with strength.

He has made the whole world so sure* that it cannot be moved;

Ever since the world began, your throne has been established;* you are from
everlasting.

The waters have lifted up, O LORD, the waters have lifted up their voice;* the waters
have lifted up their pounding waves.

Mightier than the sound of many waters, mightier than the breakers of the sea,*
mightier is the LORD who dwells on high.

Your testimonies are very sure,* and holiness adorns your house, O LORD, for ever
and for evermore.

Psalm 93

The Gloria

The Small Verse

"Behold, the days are coming, says the LORD, when I will raise up for David a
righteous Branch, and he will reign as king and deal wisely, and shall execute
justice and righteousness in the land. In his days Judah will be saved, and Israel
will dwell securely. And this is the name by which he will be called: The LORD
is our righteousness."

Jeremiah 23:5–6

The Final Thanksgiving

I will greatly rejoice in the LORD, my soul shall exult in my God; for he has clothed
me with the garments of salvation, he has covered me with the robe of
righteousness, as a bridegroom decks himself with a garland, and as a bride
adorns herself with her jewels.

Isaiah 61:10

The Petition

May the Lord GOD, father of all mercy, grant us who dwell here a peaceful night and
a perfect end. *Amen.*

꒰

Office of the Night Watch   To Be Observed on the Hour or Half Hour
Between 1:30 and 4:30 a.m.

The Call to Prayer

Behold now, bless the LORD, all you servants of the LORD,* you that stand by night
in the house of the LORD.
Lift up your hands in the holy place and bless the LORD;* the LORD who made
heaven and earth bless you out of Zion.

Psalm 134

The Request for Presence

O God, come to my assistance.
O Lord, make haste to help me.

The Greeting

Whom have I in heaven but you?* and having you I desire nothing upon earth.

Psalm 73:25

The Refrain for the Night Watch

The heavens declare the glory of God,* and the firmament shows his handiwork.
One day tells its tale to another,* and one night imparts knowledge to another.

Psalm 19:1–2

The Psalm   *Bless Him All the Day Long*

Long may he live! and may there be given to him gold from Arabia;* may prayer be
made for him always, and may they bless him all the day long.
May there be abundance of grain on the earth, growing thick even on the
hilltops;* may its fruit flourish like Lebanon, and its grain like grass upon the
earth.
May his Name remain for ever and be established as long as the sun endures;* may
all the nations bless themselves in him and call him blessed.
Blessed be the Lord GOD, the God of Israel,* who alone does wondrous deeds!
And blessed be his glorious Name for ever!* and may all the earth be filled with his
glory. Amen. Amen.

Psalm 72:15–19

The Refrain

The heavens declare the glory of God,* and the firmament shows his handiwork.
One day tells its tale to another,* and one night imparts knowledge to another.

A Reading

To all Christians—religious, clerics and laymen, men and women, to all who dwell
in the entire world, Friar Francis, their servant and subject offers submission
with reverence, true peace from Heaven, and sincere charity in the Lord.

Since I am the servant of all, I am bound to serve all and administer the sweet-
smelling words of my Lord. Whence considering in mind, that since personally
on account of the infirmity and debility of my body, I cannot visit each of you, I
have proposed by these present letters and announcements to repeat to you the
words of Our Lord Jesus Christ. . . .

Let us therefore love God and adore Him with a pure heart and a pure mind, since He
Himself, seeking such above all, has said: "True adorers will adore the Father in
spirit and in truth." *(Jn 4:23)* For "it is proper" that all, "who adore Him, adore"
Him "in the spirit of truth." *(Jn 4:24)* And let us offer Him praises and prayers
"day and night" *(Ps 31:4)* by saying, "Our Father who art in Heaven," since "it is
proper that" we "always pray and not fail to do what we might." *(Lk 18:1)*

St. Francis of Assisi, A Letter to the Faithful
(written sometime between 1216 and 1226 CE)

The Refrain

The heavens declare the glory of God,* and the firmament shows his handiwork.
One day tells its tale to another,* and one night imparts knowledge to another.

The Litany

> For all people in their daily life and work;

*For my family, friends, and neighbors, and for those who are alone, I pray to you,
Lord God.*

> For this community, the nation, and the world;

For all who work for justice, freedom, and peace, I pray to your, Lord God.

> For the just and proper use of your creation;

For the victims of hunger, fear, injustice, and oppression, I pray to you, Lord God.

> For all who are in danger, sorrow, or any kind of trouble;

*For those who minister to the sick, the friendless, and the needy, I pray to you,
Lord God.*

For the peace and unity of the Church of God;
For all who proclaim the Gospel, and all who seek the Truth, I pray to you, Lord God.
Hear me, Lord;
For your mercy is great.

The Thanksgiving

Lord, you now have set your servant free to go in peace as you have promised; for
these eyes of mine have seen the Savior whom you have prepared for all the
world to see: A Light to enlighten the nations, and the glory of your people
Israel. *Amen.*

Nunc Dimittis

The Final Petition

Now guide me waking, O Lord, and guard me sleeping; that awake I may watch with
Christ, and asleep, I may rest in peace. *Amen.*

꒰

The Office of Dawn   **To Be Observed on the Hour or Half Hour
Between 4:30 and 7:30 a.m.**

The Call to Prayer

Let everything that has breath* praise the LORD. Hallelujah!

Psalm 150:6

The Request for Presence

My soul waits for the LORD, more than watchmen for the morning,* more than
watchmen for the morning.

Psalm 130:5

The Greeting

Glory be to the Father, and to the Son, and to the Holy Spirit.
As it was in the beginning, it is now
And ever shall be, world without end. *Amen.*

Gloria Patri

The Hymn

Hail to the Lord's Anointed, great David's greater Son!
Hail in the time appointed, his reign on earth begun!
He comes to break oppression, to set the captive free;
to take away transgression, and rule in equity.

To him shall prayer unceasing and daily vows ascend;
his kingdom still increasing, a kingdom without end.
The tide of time shall never his covenant remove;
his name shall stand forever; his name to us is love.

James Montgomery

The Psalm
                                                          Praise the LORD

Hallelujah! Praise the LORD from the heavens;* praise him in the heights.
Praise him, all you angels of his;* praise him, all his host.
Praise him, sun and moon;* praise him, all you shining stars.
Praise him, heaven of heavens,* and you waters above the heavens.
Let them praise the Name of the LORD;* for he commanded, and they were
    created.
He made them stand fast for ever and ever;* he gave them a law which shall not
    pass away.

Psalm 148:1b–6

The Gloria in Excelsis

Glory to God in the highest, and on earth peace to people of good will.
    We praise you.
    We bless you.
    We adore you.
    We glorify you.
We give thanks to you for your great glory.

The Small Verse

Of John the Baptizer, Zechariah prophesied: And you, child, will be called the
    prophet of the Most High; for you will go before the Lord to prepare his ways, to
    give knowledge of salvation to his people in the forgiveness of their sins, through
    the tender mercy of our God, when the day shall dawn upon us from on high to

give light to those who sit in darkness and in the shadow of death, to guide our
feet into the way of peace.

Luke 1:76–79

The Lord's Prayer

The Final Blessing

May the Lord bless us and keep us and cause His face to shine upon us from this
day forth and forever more. *Amen.*

೭

The Morning Office   To Be Observed on the Hour or Half Hour
Between 6 and 9 a.m.

The Call to Prayer

Ascribe to the LORD the honor due his Name;* bring offerings and come into his
courts.

Psalm 96:8

The Request for Presence

I call with my whole heart; answer me, O LORD, that I may keep your statutes.

Psalm 119:145

The Greeting

Hosanna, LORD, hosanna! Lord, send us now success.

Psalm 118:25

The Refrain for the Morning Lesson

For he himself knows whereof we are made;* he remembers that we are but dust.

Psalm 103:14

A Reading

Jesus taught us saying: 'I tell you this: every thoughtless word you speak, you will
have to account for on the day of judgement. For out of your own mouth you will
be acquitted; out of your own mouth you will be condemned.'

Matthew 12:36–37

The Refrain

For he himself knows whereof we are made;* he remembers that we are but dust.

The Morning Psalm   *The Lord Has Pleasure in Those who Fear Him*

He covers the heavens with clouds* and prepares rain for the earth;

He makes grass to grow upon the mountains* and green plants to serve mankind.

He provides food for flocks and herds* and for the young ravens when they cry.

He is not impressed by the might of a horse;* he has no pleasure in the strength of a man;

But the Lord has pleasure in those who fear him,* in those who await his gracious favor.

Psalm 147:8–12

The Refrain

For he himself knows whereof we are made;* he remembers that we are but dust.

The Gloria

The Lord's Prayer

The Prayer Appointed for the Day

Hasten, O Father, the coming of your kingdom; and grant that all who now live by your faith, may with joy behold your Son at his coming in glorious majesty; even Jesus Christ, our only Mediator and Advocate. *Amen.*

The Concluding Prayer of the Church

Lord God, almighty and everlasting Father, you have brought me in safety to the beginning of this day: Preserve me with your mighty power, that I may not fall into sin, nor be overcome by adversity; and in all I do, direct me to the fulfilling of your purposes; through Jesus Christ my Lord. *Amen.*

The Midday Office   **To Be Observed on the Hour or Half Hour**
                                              Between 11 a.m. and 2 p.m.

The Call to Prayer
Open my lips, O Lord,* and my mouth shall proclaim your praise.

Psalm 51:16

The Request for Presence
You are my crag and my stronghold;* for the sake of your Name, lead me and
    guide me.

Psalm 31:3

The Greeting
May God give his blessing,* and may all the ends of the earth stand in awe of him.

Psalm 67:7

The Refrain for the Midday Lessons
Happy are the people whose strength is in you!* whose hearts are set on the
    pilgrim's way.

Psalm 84:4

A Reading
Always be joyful; pray continually; give thanks whatever happens; for this is what
    God wills for you in Christ Jesus.

1 Thessalonians 5:16–18

The Refrain
Happy are the people whose strength is in you!* whose hearts are set on the
    pilgrim's way.

The Midday Psalm   *How Priceless Is Your Love, O God*
Your love, O LORD, reaches to the heavens,* and your faithfulness to the clouds.
Your righteousness is like the strong mountains, your justice like the great deep;*
    you save both man and beast, O LORD.
How priceless is your love, O God!* your people take refuge under the shadow of
    your wings.

They feast upon the abundance of your house;* you give them drink from the river of your delights.
For with you is the well of life,* and in your light we see light.
Continue your loving-kindness to those who know you,* and your favor to those who are true of heart.

Psalm 36:5–10

The Refrain
Happy are the people whose strength is in you!* whose hearts are set on the pilgrim's way.

The Gloria

The Lord's Prayer

The Prayer Appointed for the Day
Hasten, O Father, the coming of your kingdom; and grant that all who now live by your faith, may with joy behold your Son at his coming in glorious majesty; even Jesus Christ, our only Mediator and Advocate. *Amen.*

The Concluding Prayer of the Church
Lord Jesus Christ, by your death you took away the sting of death: Grant me to so follow in faith where you have led the way, that I may at length fall asleep peacefully in you and wake in your likeness; for your tender mercies' sake. *Amen.*

༄

The Vespers Office   **To Be Observed on the Hour or Half Hour Between 5 and 8 p.m.**

The Call to Prayer
Know this: The LORD himself is God;* he himself has made us, and we are his; we are his people and the sheep of his pasture.

Psalm 100:2

59

The Request for Presence

O LORD, let my prayer be set forth in your sight as incense, the lifting up of my
hands as the evening sacrifice.

Psalm 141:2, adapted

The Greeting

Our Father, forgive us our sins as we forgive those who have sinned against us..

The Hymn

Blessed be the tie that binds
our hearts in Christian love;
the fellowship of kindred minds
is like to that above.

We share each other's woes
our mutual burdens bear;
and often for each other flow
the sympathizing tear.

Before our Father's throne,
we pour our ardent prayers;
our fears, our hopes, our aims are one,
our comforts and our cares

When we asunder part,
it gives us inward pain;
but we shall still be joined in heart,
and hope to meet again.

John Fawcett

The Refrain for the Vespers Lessons

I will fulfill my vows to the LORD* in the presence of all his people.

Psalm 116:16

The Vespers Psalm   *Light Shines in the Darkness for the Upright*

Light shines in the darkness for the upright;* the righteous are merciful and full of
compassion.

It is good for them to be generous in lending* and to manage their affairs with justice.

For they will never be shaken;* the righteous will be kept in everlasting
    remembrance.

They will not be afraid of any evil rumors;* their heart is right; they put their trust in
    the Lord.

Their heart is established and will not shrink,

Psalm 112:4–8a

The Refrain

I will fulfill my vows to the LORD* in the presence of all his people.

The Gloria

The Lord's Prayer

The Prayer Appointed for the Day

Hasten, O Father, the coming of your kingdom; and grant that all who now live by
    your faith, may with joy behold your Son at his coming in glorious majesty; even
    Jesus Christ, our only Mediator and Advocate. *Amen.*

The Concluding Prayer of the Church

Heavenly Father, in you I live and move and have my being; I humbly pray you so to
    guide and govern me by your Holy Spirit, that in all the cares and occupations of
    my life I may not forget you, but may remember that I am ever walking in your
    sight; through Jesus Christ my Lord. *Amen.*

The Office of Compline   To Be Observed Before Retiring

The Call to Prayer

May the Lord Almighty grant me and those I love a peaceful night and a perfect end.
    Amen.

The Request for Presence

Our help is in the Name of the Lord; the maker of heaven and earth.

The Greeting

Almighty God, my heavenly Father, I have sinned against you, through my own fault in thought, and word, and deed, in what I have done and what I have left undone. For the sake of your Son our Lord Jesus Christ, forgive me all my offenses; and grant that I may serve you in newness of life, to the glory of your Name. *Amen.*

The Reading   *The Nicene Creed*

We believe in one God, the Father, the Almighty, maker of heaven and earth, of all that is, seen and unseen. We believe in one Lord, Jesus Christ. The only Son of God, eternally begotten of the Father, God from God, Light from Light, true God from true God, begotten, not made, of one Being with the Father. Through him all things were made. For us and for our salvation he came down from heaven: by the power of the Holy Spirit he became incarnate from the Virgin Mary, and was made man. For our sake he was crucified under Pontius Pilate; he suffered death and was buried. On the third day he rose again in accordance with the Scriptures; he ascended into heaven and is seated at the right hand of the Father. He will come again in glory to judge the living and the dead, and his kingdom shall have no end. We believe in the Holy Spirit, the Lord, the giver of life, who proceeds from the Father and the Son. With the Father and the Son he is worshiped and glorified. He has spoken through the Prophets. We believe in one holy, catholic and apostolic Church. We acknowledge one baptism for the forgiveness of sins. We look for the resurrection of the dead, and the life of the world to come. *Amen.*

The Gloria

The Psalm   *The LORD Will Save Those Whose Spirits Are Crushed*

The eyes of the LORD are upon the righteous,* and his ears are open to their cry.

The face of the LORD is against those who do evil,* to root out the remembrance of them from the earth.

The righteous cry, and the LORD hears them* and delivers them from all their troubles.

The LORD is near to the brokenhearted* and will save those whose spirits are crushed.

Many are the troubles of the righteous,* but the LORD will deliver him out of them all.

He will keep safe all his bones;* not one of them shall be broken.
Evil shall slay the wicked,* and those who hate the righteous will be punished.
The LORD ransoms the life of his servants,* and none will be punished who trust
    in him.

Psalm 34:15–22

The Gloria

The Small Verse

Into your hands, O Lord, I commend my spirit; For you have redeemed me, O Lord,
    O God of truth. Keep me, O Lord, as the apple of your eye; Hide me under the
    shadow of your wings.

The Lord's Prayer

The Petition

Lord, hear my prayers; and let my cry come to you.

The Final Thanksgiving

Lord, you now have set your servant free to go in peace as you have promised; for
    these eyes of mine have seen the Savior, whom you have prepared for all the
    world to see: a Light to enlighten the nations, and the glory of your people Israel.
    Glory to the Father, and to the Son, and to the Holy Spirit: as it was in the
    beginning, is now, and ever more shall be. *Amen.*

THURSDAY

The Office of Midnight **To Be Observed on the Hour or Half Hour**
Between 10:30 p.m.✧ and 1:30 a.m.

The Call to Prayer
Worship the LORD in the beauty of holiness;* let the whole earth tremble before him.

Psalm 96:9

The Request for Presence
O LORD, let my prayer be set forth in your sight as incense,* the lifting up of my
    hands as the evening sacrifice.

Psalm 141:2

The Greeting
Our Father, Yours are the kingdom, the power, and the glory forever.

The Canticle **The Song of Zechariah**
Benedictus Dominus Deus

Blessed be the Lord, the God of Israel;*
    he has come to his people and set them free.
He has raised up for us a mighty savior,*
    born of the house of his servant David
You, my child, shall be called the prophet of the Most High,*
    for you will go before the Lord to prepare his way,
To give his people knowledge of salvation*
    by the forgiveness of their sins.
In the tender compassion of our God*
    the dawn from on high shall break upon us,
To shine on those who dwell in darkness and the shadow of death,*
    and to guide our feet into the way of peace.
Glory to the Father, and to the Son, and to the Holy Spirit:*
    as it was in the beginning, is now, and will be for ever. *Amen.*

Luke 1:68–69, 76–79

The Psalm **God Sits upon His Holy Throne**
Clap your hands, all you peoples;* shout to God with a cry of joy.
God has gone up with a shout,* the LORD with the sound of the ram's-horn.
Sing praises to God, sing praises;* sing praises to our King, sing praises.

For God is King of all the earth;* sing praises with all your skill.
God reigns over the nations;* God sits upon his holy throne.
The nobles of the peoples have gathered together* with the people of the God of Abraham.
The rulers of the earth belong to God,* and he is highly exalted.

Psalm 47:1, 5–10

The Gloria

The Small Verse
So faith, hope, love abide, these three; but the greatest of these is love.

1 Corinthians 13:13

The Final Thanksgiving
I will greatly rejoice in the LORD, my soul shall exult in my God; for he has clothed me with the garments of salvation, he has covered me with the robe of righteousness, as a bridegroom decks himself with a garland, and as a bride adorns herself with her jewels.

Isaiah 61:10

The Petition
May the Lord GOD, father of grace and mercy, grant all who dwell here a peaceful night and a perfect end. *Amen.*

౩

Office of the Night Watch   To Be Observed on the Hour or Half Hour Between 1:30 and 4:30 a.m.

The Call to Prayer
Behold now, bless the LORD, all you servants of the LORD,* you that stand by night in the house of the LORD.
Lift up your hands in the holy place and bless the LORD;* the LORD who made heaven and earth bless you out of Zion.

Psalm 134

67

The Request for Presence

O God, come to my assistance.
O Lord, make haste to help me.

The Greeting

"You are my God, and I will thank you;* you are my God, and I will exalt you."

Psalm 118:28

The Refrain for the Night Watch

It is a good thing to give thanks to the LORD,* and to sing praises to your Name, O
   Most High;
To tell of your loving-kindness early in the morning* and of your faithfulness in the
   night season.

Psalm 92:1–2

The Psalm   LORD, I Am Your Servant

LORD, I am your servant;* I am your servant and the child of your handmaid; you
   have freed me from my bonds.
I will offer you the sacrifice of thanksgiving* and call upon the Name of the LORD.
I will fulfill my vows to the LORD* in the presence of all his people,
In the courts of the LORD's house,* in the midst of you, O Jerusalem. Hallelujah!

Psalm 116:14–17

The Refrain

It is a good thing to give thanks to the LORD,* and to sing praises to your Name, O
   Most High;
To tell of your loving-kindness early in the morning* and of your faithfulness in the
   night season.

A Reading

Let your children be partakers of true Christian training; let them learn of how great
   avail humility is with God(how much the spirit of pure affection can prevail with
   Him(how excellent and great His fear is, and how it saves all those who walk in
   it with a pure mind. For He is a Searcher of the thoughts and desires [of the
   heart]: His breath is in us; and when He pleases, He will take it away.

Clement of Rome (ca. 57 CE), 1st Epistle of Clement to the Corinthians, XXI, 94–95

The Refrain

It is a good thing to give thanks to the LORD,* and to sing praises to your Name,
O Most High;
To tell of your loving-kindness early in the morning* and of your faithfulness in the
night season.

The Litany

For the peace from above, for the loving-kindness of God, and for the salvation of
my soul, I pray to the Lord.
Lord, have mercy.
For the peace of the world, for the welfare of the Holy Church of God, and for the
unity of all peoples, I pray to the Lord.
Lord, have mercy.
For my city (town, village), for every city and community, and for those who live in
them, I pray to the Lord.
Lord, have mercy.
For seasonable weather, and for an abundance of the fruits of the earth, I pray to
the Lord.
Lord, have mercy.
For the good earth which God has given us, and for the wisdom and will to conserve
it, I pray to the Lord.
Lord, have mercy.
For deliverance from all danger, violence, oppression, and degradation, I pray to
the Lord.
Lord, have mercy.
For the absolution and remission of my sins and offenses, I pray to the Lord.
Lord, have mercy.
Defend me, deliver me, and in your compassion protect me, O Lord, by your grace.
Lord, have mercy.

The Thanksgiving

Lord, you now have set your servant free to go in peace as you have promised; for
these eyes of mine have seen the Savior whom you have prepared for all the
world to see: A Light to enlighten the nations, and the glory of your people
Israel. *Amen.*

Nunc Dimittis

69

The Final Petition

Now guide me waking, O Lord, and guard me sleeping; that awake I may watch with
Christ, and asleep, I may rest in peace. *Amen.*

౨౨

The Office of Dawn **To Be Observed on the Hour or Half Hour**
Between 4:30 and 7:30 a.m.

The Call to Prayer

Worship the Lord, O Jerusalem;* praise your God, O Zion;
For he has strengthened the bars of your gates.

Psalm 147:13–14a

The Request for Presence

My soul waits for the Lord, more than watchmen for the morning,* more than
watchmen for the morning.

Psalm 130:5

The Greeting

Glory be to the Father, and the Son, and the Holy Spirit.
As it was in the beginning, it is now
And ever shall be, world without end. *Amen.*

The Hymn

O love, how deep, how broad, how high,
it fills the heart with ecstasy,
that God, the Son of God, should take
our mortal form for mortals' sake!

For us he prayed; for us he taught;
for us his daily works he wrought;
by words and signs and actions thus
still seeking not himself, but us.

All glory to our Lord and God
for love so deep, so high, so broad;
the Trinity whom we adore,
forever and forevermore.

15th c. Latin, translated by Benjamin Webb

The Psalm   *The LORD Takes Pleasure in His People*

Let Israel rejoice in his Maker;* let the children of Zion be joyful in their King.
Let them praise his Name in the dance;* let them sing praise to him with timbrel
    and harp.
For the LORD takes pleasure in his people* and adorns the poor with victory.
Let the faithful rejoice in triumph;* let them be joyful on their beds.

Psalm 149:2–5

The Gloria in Excelsis

Glory to God in the highest, and on earth peace to people of good will.
    We praise you.
    We bless you.
    We adore you.
    We glorify you.
We give thanks to you for your great glory.

The Small Verse

Jesus taught us, saying: "If you love me, you will keep my commandments. And I will
    pray the Father, and he will give you another Counselor, to be with you forever,
    even the Spirit of truth, whom the world cannot receive, because it neither sees
    him nor knows him; you know him, for he dwells with you, and will be in you."

John 14:15–16

The Lord's Prayer

The Final Blessing

May the LORD bless us and keep us and cause His face to shine upon us from this
    day forth and forever more. *Amen.*

The Morning Office   **To Be Observed on the Hour or Half Hour**
Between 6 and 9 a.m.

The Call to Prayer

Hallelujah! Praise the LORD from the heavens;* praise him in the heights.

Psalm 148:1

The Request for Presence

My soul waits for the LORD, more than watchmen for the morning,* more than
   watchmen for the morning.

Psalm 130:5

The Greeting

You are worthy, O Lord our God, to receive glory and honour and power, because
   you created all things; by your will they were created and have their being.

Revelation 4:11

The Refrain for the Morning Lessons

Bless the LORD, O my soul,* and all that is within me, bless his holy Name.

Psalm 103:1

A Reading

Yet another said, 'I will follow you, sir; but let me first say good-bye to my people at
   home.' To him Jesus said, 'No one who sets his hand to the plough and then
   looks back is fit for the kingdom of God.'

Luke 9:61–62

The Refrain

Bless the LORD, O my soul,* and all that is within me, bless his holy Name.

The Morning Psalm   *Teach Us To Number Our Days*

Lord, you have been our refuge* from one generation to another.
Before the mountains were brought forth, or the land and the earth were born,* from
   age to age you are God.
You turn us back to the dust and say,* "Go back, O child of earth."
For a thousand years in your sight are like yesterday when it is past* and like a
   watch in the night.
You sweep us away like a dream;* we fade away suddenly like the grass.

In the morning it is green and flourishes;* in the evening it is dried up and withered.

For we consume away in your displeasure;* we are afraid because of your wrathful indignation.

Our iniquities you have set before you,* and our secret sins in the light of your countenance.

So teach us to number our days* that we may apply our hearts to wisdom.

Psalm 90:1–8, 12

The Refrain

Bless the LORD, O my soul,* and all that is within me, bless his holy Name.

The Gloria

The Lord's Prayer

The Prayer Appointed for the Day

O Lord, you have taught us that without love whatever we do is worth nothing: Send your Holy Spirit and pour into my heart your greatest gift which is love, the true bond of peace and of all virtue without which whoever lives is accounted dead before you. Grant this for the sake of your only Son Jesus Christ, who lives and reigns with you and the Holy Spirit, one God, now and for ever. *Amen.*

The Concluding Prayer of the Church

Lord God, almighty and everlasting Father, you have brought me in safety to the beginning of his day: Preserve me with your mighty power, that I may not fall into sin, nor be overcome by adversity; and in all I do, direct me to the fulfilling of your purposes; through Jesus Christ my Lord. *Amen.*

∾

The Midday Office

To Be Observed on the Hour or Half Hour Between 11 a.m. and 2 p.m.

The Call to Prayer

Bless the LORD, O my soul,*and all that is within me, bless his holy Name.

Bless the LORD, O my soul,*and forget not all his benefits.

Psalm 103:1–2

The Request for Presence

Show your goodness, O LORD, to those who are good* and to those who are true of heart.

Psalm 124:4

The Greeting

You have set a banner for those who fear you* . . .
Save us by your right hand and answer us.*

Psalm 60: 4–5

The Refrain for the Midday Lessons

Let all the earth fear the LORD;* let all who dwell in the world stand in awe of him.

Psalm 33:8

A Reading

Then a branch will grow from the stock of Jesse, and a shoot will spring from his roots. On him the spirit of the LORD will rest: a spirit of wisdom and understanding, a spirit of counsel and power, a spirit of knowledge and fear of the LORD; and in the fear of the LORD will be his delight. He will not judge by outward appearances or decide a case on hearsay; but with justice he will judge the poor and defend the humble in the land of equity; like a rod his verdict will strike the ruthless, and with his word he will slay the wicked. He will wear the belt of justice, and truth shall be his girdle.

Isaiah 11:1–5

The Refrain

Let all the earth fear the LORD;* let all who dwell in the world stand in awe of him.

The Midday Psalm   Let Everything That Has Breath Praise the LORD

Praise him for his mighty acts;* praise him for his excellent greatness.
Praise him with the blast of the ram's-horn;* praise him with lyre and harp.
Praise him with timbrel and dance;* praise him with strings and pipe.
Praise him with resounding cymbals;* praise him with loud-clanging cymbals.
Let everything that has breath* praise the LORD. Hallelujah!

Psalm 150:2–6

The Refrain
Let all the earth fear the LORD;* let all who dwell in the world stand in awe
of him.

The Gloria

The Lord's Prayer

The Prayer Appointed for the Day
O Lord, you have taught us that without love whatever we do is worth nothing:
Send your Holy Spirit and pour into my heart your greatest gift which is love,
the true bond of peace and of all virtue without which whoever lives is
accounted dead before you. Grant this for the sake of your only Son Jesus
Christ, who lives and reigns with you and the Holy Spirit, one God, now and
for ever. *Amen.*

The Concluding Prayer of the Church
Almighty God, who has promised to hear the petitions of those who ask in your
Son's name: I beseech you mercifully to incline your ear to me who have made
my prayers and supplications to you; and grant that those things which I have
faithfully asked according to your will, may effectually be obtained, to the relief
of my necessity, and to the setting forth of your glory, through Jesus Christ my
Lord. *Amen.*

ॐ

The Vespers Office   To Be Observed on the Hour or Half Hour
                                          Between 5 and 8 p.m.

The Call to Prayer
Let us come before his presence with thanksgiving*and raise a loud shout to him.

Psalm 95:2

The Request for Presence
Show me the light of your countenance, O God, and come to me.

Psalm 67:1, adapted

75

The Greeting

You are my God, and I will thank you;* you are my God and I will exalt you.

Psalm 118:28

The Hymn   He–Psalm 119:33–40

Help me, O Lord, Your law to see
that I may keep it endlessly.
Make me discern Your holy way;
preserve it in my heart today.

Cause me to walk by Your command
along the path to take Your hand.
And turn my heart from unjust gain,
and turn my eyes from all that's vain.

Give life to me in Your just way
and raise Your servant up today.
Utter Your word so I may hear.
Pass over the reproach I fear.

Behold, I long for what is good,
I long to follow as I should.
Revive my heart to set it right.
Show me, O Lord, my soul's delight.

Margaret B. Ingraham, THIS HOLY ALPHABET (HE is the fifth letter
of the Hebrew alphabet) May be sung to the tune of Tallis' Canon

The Refrain for the Vespers Lessons

Search for the LORD and his strength;* continually seek his face.

Psalm 105:4

The Vespers Psalm   Happy Are They Whose Hope Is in the LORD Their God

Happy are they who have the God of Jacob for their help!* whose hope is in the
    LORD their God;
Who made heaven and earth, the seas, and all that is in them;* who keeps his
    promise for ever;
Who gives justice to those who are oppressed,* and food to those who hunger.

76

The LORD loves the righteous; the LORD cares for the stranger,* he sustains the
    orphan and widow, but frustrates the way of the wicked.
The LORD shall reign for ever,* your God, O Zion, throughout all generations.
    Hallelujah!

Psalm 146:4–6, 8–9

The Refrain
Search for the LORD and his strength;* continually seek his face.

The Gloria

The Lord's Prayer

The Prayer Appointed for the Day
O Lord, you have taught us that without love whatever we do is worth nothing: Send
    your Holy Spirit and pour into my heart your greatest gift which is love, the true
    bond of peace and of all virtue without which whoever lives is accounted dead
    before you. Grant this for the sake of your only Son Jesus Christ, who lives and
    reigns with you and the Holy Spirit, one God, now and for ever. *Amen.*

The Concluding Prayer of the Church
Lord Jesus, stay with me, for evening is at hand and the day is past; be my
    companion in the way, kindle my heart, and awaken hope, that I may know you
    as you are revealed in Scripture and the breaking of bread. Grant this for the sake
    of your love. *Amen.*

The Office of Compline   To Be Observed Before Retiring

The Call to Prayer
May the Lord Almighty grant me and those I love a peaceful night and a perfect end.
    Amen.

The Request for Presence
Our help is in the Name of the Lord; the maker of heaven and earth.

The Greeting

Almighty God, my heavenly Father, I have sinned against you, through my own fault
in thought, and word, and deed, in what I have done and what I have left undone.
For the sake of your Son our Lord Jesus Christ, forgive me all my offenses; and
grant that I may serve you in newness of life, to the glory of your Name. *Amen.*

The Reading

We do not know—nor can we tell—what the essence of God is; or how it is that it
should be in all; or how the Only-Begotten Son and God, having emptied
Himself, became Man, born of virgin blood and made by another law contrary to
nature; or even how He walked with dry feet upon the waters.
It is not within our capacity, therefore, to say anything about God(or even to think of
Him(beyond those things which have been divinely revealed to us, whether by
word or by manifestations or by the divine oracles at once of the Old Testament
and the New.

John of Damascus (ca. 760 CE), An Exact Exposition of the Orthodox Faith

The Gloria

The Psalm   *Create in Me a Clean Heart*

Create in me a clean heart, O God,* and renew a right spirit within me.
Cast me not away from your presence* and take not your holy Spirit from me.
Give me the joy of your saving help again* and sustain me with your bountiful
Spirit.
I shall teach your ways to the wicked,* and sinners shall return to you.

Psalm 51:11–14

The Gloria

The Small Verse

Into your hands, O Lord, I commend my spirit; For you have redeemed me, O Lord,
O God of truth. Keep me, O Lord, as the apple of your eye; Hide me under the
shadow of your wings.

The Lord's Prayer

The Petition

Keep watch, dear Lord, with those who work, or watch, or weep this night, and give your angels charge over those who sleep. Tend the sick, Lord Christ; give rest to the weary, bless the dying, soothe the suffering, pity the afflicted, shield the joyous; and all for your love's sake. *Amen.*

The Final Thanksgiving

Lord, you now have set your servant free to go in peace as you have promised; for these eyes of mine have seen the Savior, whom you have prepared for all the world to see: a Light to enlighten the nations, and the glory of your people Israel. Glory to the Father, and to the Son, and to the Holy Spirit: as it was in the beginning, is now, and ever more shall be. *Amen.*

FRIDAY

The Office of Midnight   **To Be Observed on the Hour or Half Hour**
Between 10:30 p.m.✧ and 1:30 a.m.

The Call to Prayer

Let the Name of the LORD be blessed,* from this time forth for evermore.
From the rising of the sun to its going down* let the Name of the LORD be
   praised.

Psalm 113:2–3

The Request for Presence

O Lord, let my prayer be set forth in your sight as incense,* the lifting up of my
   hands as the evening sacrifice

Psalm 141:2, adapted

The Greeting

Our Father Who art in Heaven, hallowed be Your name.

The Canticle   *The Song of Moses*
                                                   Cantemus Domino

I will sing to the Lord, for he is lofty and uplifted;*
   the horse and its rider has he hurled into the sea.
The Lord is my strength and my refuge;*
   the Lord has become my Savior.
This is my God and I will praise him,*
   the God of my people and I will exalt him.
The Lord is a mighty warrior;*
   Yahweh is his Name.
Who can be compared with you, O Lord, among the gods?*
   who is like you, glorious in holiness, awesome in renown, and worker of
      wonders?
With your constant love you led the people you redeemed;*
   with your might you brought them in safety to your holy dwelling.
You will bring them in and plant them*
   on the mount of your possession,
The resting-place you have made for yourself, O Lord,*
   the sanctuary, O Lord, that your hand has established.
The Lord shall reign*
   for ever and for ever.

Exodus 15:1–6, 11–13, 17–18

The Psalm   *All His Commandments Are Sure*

Hallelujah! I will give thanks to the LORD with my whole heart,* in the assembly of
the upright, in the congregation.

Great are the deeds of the LORD!* they are studied by all who delight in them.

His work is full of majesty and splendor,* and his righteousness endures for ever.

The works of his hands are faithfulness and justice;* all his commandments are sure.

They stand fast for ever and ever,* because they are done in truth and equity.

He sent redemption to his people; he commanded his covenant for ever;* holy and
awesome is his Name.

The fear of the LORD is the beginning of wisdom;* those who act accordingly have a
good understanding; his praise endures for ever.

Psalm 111:1–3, 7–10

The Gloria

The Small Verse

The sun shall be no more your light by day, nor for brightness shall the moon give
light to you by night; but the LORD will be your everlasting light, and your God
will be your glory.

Isaiah 60:19

The Final Thanksgiving

I will greatly rejoice in the LORD, my soul shall exult in my God; for he has
clothed me with the garments of salvation, he has covered me with the robe
of righteousness, as a bridegroom decks himself with a garland, and as a bride
adorns herself with her jewels.

Isaiah 61:10

The Petition

May the Lord GOD, father of all mercy, grant us who dwell here a peaceful night and
a perfect end. *Amen.*

Office of the Night Watch   To Be Observed on the Hour or Half Hour
Between 1:30 and 4:30 a.m.

The Call to Prayer
Behold now, bless the LORD, all you servants of the LORD,* you that stand by night
    in the house of the LORD.
Lift up your hands in the holy place and bless the LORD;* the LORD who made
    heaven and earth bless you out of Zion.

Psalm 134

The Request for Presence
O God, come to my assistance.
O Lord, make haste to help me.

The Greeting
"You are my God, and I will thank you;* you are my God, and I will exalt you."

Psalm 118:28

The Refrain for the Night Watch
You shall not be afraid of any terror by night,* nor of the arrow that flies
    by day;

Psalm 91:5

The Psalm   *Your Word Is Everlasting*
In your loving-kindness, revive me,* that I may keep the decrees of your mouth.
O LORD, your word is everlasting;* it stands firm in the heavens.
Your faithfulness remains from one generation to another;* you established the
    earth, and it abides.
By your decree these continue to this day,* for all things are your servants.
If my delight had not been in your law,* I should have perished in my affliction.
I will never forget your commandments,* because by them you give me life.
I am yours; oh, that you would save me!* for I study your commandments.

Psalm 119:88–94

The Refrain
You shall not be afraid of any terror by night,* nor of the arrow that flies by day;

84

A Reading

All our power is of God; I say *of God!* From Him we have life; from Him we have strength; by power derived and conceived from Him, we do, while yet in this world, foreknow the indications of things to come. Only remember, let fear be the keeper of innocence in order that the Lord, who of His mercy has flowed into our hearts in an access of celestial grace, may be kept by righteous submissiveness in the hostelry of a grateful mind so that the assurance we have gained may not beget carelessness, and the old enemy creep up on us again.

Cyprian, Bishop of Carthage (d. ca. 258), The Epistles

The Refrain

You shall not be afraid of any terror by night,* nor of the arrow that flies by day;

The Litany

Grant, Almighty God, that all who confess your Name may be united in your truth, live together in your love, and reveal your glory in the world.

Lord, in your mercy, hear my prayer.

Guide the people of this land, and of all the nations, in the ways of justice and peace; that we may honor one another and serve the common good.

Lord, in your mercy, hear my prayer.

Give us all a reverence for the earth as your own creation, that we may use its resources rightly in the service of others and to your honor and glory.

Lord, in your mercy, hear my prayer.

Bless all whose lives are closely linked with mine, and grant that I may serve Christ in them, and love even as he loves me.

Lord, in your mercy, hear my prayer.

Comfort and heal all those who suffer in body, mind, or spirit; give them courage and hope in their troubles, and bring them the joy of your salvation.

Lord, in your mercy, hear my prayer.

I commend to your mercy all who have died, that your will for them may be fulfilled; and I pray that I may share with all your saints in your eternal kingdom.

Lord, in your mercy, hear my prayer.

The Thanksgiving

Lord, you now have set your servant free to go in peace as you have promised; for these eyes of mine have seen the Savior whom you have prepared for all the world to see: A Light to enlighten the nations, and the glory of your people Israel. *Amen.*

Nunc Dimittis

The Final Petition

Now guide me waking, O Lord, and guard me sleeping; that awake I may watch with Christ, and asleep, I may rest in peace. *Amen.*

༈

The Office of Dawn **To Be Observed on the Hour or Half Hour Between 4:30 and 7:30 a.m.**

The Call to Prayer

Let everything that has breath* praise the LORD. Hallelujah!

Psalm 150:6

The Request for Presence

My soul waits for the LORD, more than watchmen for the morning,* more than watchmen for the morning.

Psalm 130:5

The Greeting

Glory be to the Father, and the Son, and the Holy Spirit.
As it was in the beginning, it is now
And ever shall be, world without end. *Amen.*

Gloria Patri

The Hymn

God moves in a mysterious way
His wonders to perform;
He plants his footsteps in the sea,
And rides upon the storm.

Deep in unfathomable mines
Of never-failing skill,
He treasures up his bright designs,
And works his sovereign will.

You fearful saints, fresh courage take,
The clouds you so much dread
Are big with mercy, and shall break
In blessings on your head.

William Cowper

The Psalm   *Let Everything that Has Breath Praise the L*ORD**

Praise him for his mighty acts;* praise him for his excellent greatness.
Praise him with the blast of the ram's-horn;* praise him with lyre and harp.
Praise him with timbrel and dance;* praise him with strings and pipe.
Praise him with resounding cymbals;* praise him with loud-clanging cymbals.
Let everything that has breath* praise the Lord. Hallelujah!

Psalm 150:2–6

The Gloria in Excelsis

Glory to God in the highest, and on earth peace to people of good will.
 We praise you.
 We bless you.
 We adore you.
 We glorify you.
We give thanks to you for your great glory.

The Small Verse

The cup of blessing which we bless, is it not a participation in the blood of Christ?
 The bread which we break, is it not a participation in the body of Christ?
 Because there is one bread, we who are many are one body, for we all partake of
 the one bread.

1 Corinthians 10:16–17

The Lord's Prayer

The Final Blessing
May the LORD bless us and keep us and cause His face to shine upon us from this
day forth and forever more. *Amen.*

$\backsim$

The Morning Office   **To Be Observed on the Hour or Half Hour
Between 6 and 9 a.m.**

The Call to Prayer
Worship the LORD, O Jerusalem;* praise your God, O Zion;
For he has strengthened the bars of your gates.

Psalm 147:13–14a

The Request for Presence
My soul waits for the LORD, more than watchmen for the morning,* more than
watchmen for the morning.

Psalm 130:5

The Greeting
Glory be to the Father, and the Son, and the Holy Spirit.
As it was in the beginning, it is now
And ever shall be, world without end. *Amen.*

The Refrain for the Morning Lessons
The human mind and heart are a mystery; but God will loose an arrow at them,* and
suddenly they will be wounded.

Psalm 164:7

A Reading
Jesus taught us, saying: 'Be on your guard; do not let your minds be dulled by
dissipation and drunkenness and worldly cares so that the great day catches you
suddenly like a trap; for that day will come on everyone, the whole world over.

Be on the alert, praying at all times for strength to pass safely through all that is coming and to stand in the presence of the Son of Man.'

Luke 21:34–36

The Refrain

The human mind and heart are a mystery; but God will loose an arrow at them,* and suddenly they will be wounded.

The Morning Psalm   The LORD, My Refuge and My Stronghold

He who dwells in the shelter of the Most High,* abides under the shadow of the Almighty.

He shall say to the LORD, "You are my refuge and my stronghold,* my God in whom I put my trust."

He shall deliver you from the snare of the hunter* and from the deadly pestilence.

He shall cover you with his pinions, and you shall find refuge under his wings;* his faithfulness shall be a shield and buckler.

You shall not be afraid of any terror by night,* nor of the arrow that flies by day;

Of the plague that stalks in the darkness,* nor of the sickness that lays waste at mid-day.

A thousand shall fall at your side and ten thousand at your right hand,* but it shall not come near you.

Psalm 91:1–7

The Refrain

The human mind and heart are a mystery; but God will loose an arrow at them,* and suddenly they will be wounded.

The Gloria

The Lord's Prayer

The Prayer Appointed for the Day

Almighty and everlasting God, by whose Spirit the whole body of your faithful people is governed and sanctified: Receive my supplications and prayers, which I offer before you for all members of your holy Church, that in our vocations and ministries we may truly and devoutly serve you; through our Lord and Savior Jesus Christ, who lives and reigns with you, in the unity of the Holy Spirit, one God, now and forever. *Amen.*

89

The Concluding Prayer of the Church

Lord God, almighty and everlasting Father, you have brought me in safety to the beginning of this day: Preserve me with your mighty power, that I may not fall into sin, nor be overcome by adversity; and in all I do, direct me to the fulfilling of your purposes; through Jesus Christ my Lord. *Amen.*

༈

The Midday Office   To Be Observed on the Hour or Half Hour Between 11 a.m. and 2 p.m.

The Call to Prayer

Love the LORD, all you who worship him;* the LORD protects the faithful, but repays to the full those who act haughtily.

Psalm 31:24

The Request for Presence

O God, come to my assistance.
O Lord, make haste to help me.

The Greeting

Blessed is the LORD!* for he has heard the voice of my prayer.

Psalm 28:7

The Refrain for the Midday Lessons

The LORD is near to those who call upon him,* to all who call upon him faithfully.

Psalm 146:19

A Reading

Our transgressions against you are many, and our sins bear witness against us; our transgressions are on our minds, and well we know our guilt: we have rebelled and broken faith with the LORD, we have relapsed and forsaken our God; we have conceived lies on our hearts and repeated them in slanderous and treacherous words. Justice is rebuffed and flouted while righteousness stands at a distance; truth stumbles in court and honesty is kept outside, so truth is lost to sight, and those who shun evil withdraw.

Isaiah 59:12–15

The Refrain
The LORD is near to those who call upon him,* to all who call upon him faithfully.

The Midday Psalm   Wait Patiently for the LORD
Hearken to my voice, O LORD, when I call;* have mercy on me and answer me.
You speak in my heart and say, "Seek my face."* Your face, LORD, will I seek.
Hide not your face from me,* nor turn away your servant in displeasure.
What if I had not believed that I should see the goodness of the LORD* in the land of the living!
O tarry and await the LORD's pleasure; be strong, and he shall comfort your heart;* wait patiently for the LORD.

Psalm 27:10–12 ff

The Refrain
The LORD is near to those who call upon him,* to all who call upon him faithfully.

The Gloria

The Lord's Prayer

The Prayer Appointed for the Day
Almighty and everlasting God, by whose Spirit the whole body of your faithful people is governed and sanctified: Receive my supplications and prayers, which I offer before you for all members of your holy Church, that in our vocations and ministries we may truly and devoutly serve you; through our Lord and Savior Jesus Christ, who lives and reigns with you, in the unity of the Holy Spirit, one God, now and forever. *Amen.*

The Concluding Prayer of the Church
O merciful Creator, your hand is open wide to satisfy the needs of every living creature: Make me always thankful for your loving providence; and grant that remembering the account I must one day give, I may be a faithful steward of

your good gifts; through Jesus Christ our Lord, who with you and the Holy Spirit lives and reigns, one God, for ever and ever. *Amen.*

࠾

The Vespers Office   **To Be Observed on the Hour or Half Hour Between 5 and 8 p.m.**

The Call to Prayer
Worship the LORD in the beauty of holiness;* let the whole earth tremble before him.

Psalm 96:9

The Request for Presence
O LORD, let my prayer be set forth in your sight as incense,* the lifting up of my hands as the evening sacrifice.

Psalm 141:2

The Greeting
Lord, have mercy on me. Christ, have mercy on me. Lord, have mercy on me.

The Hymn
Pass me not, O gentle Savior,
Hear my humble cry;
While on others You are calling
Do not pass me by.
Savior, Savior, hear my humble cry.

Trusting only in Your merit,
Would I seek Your face;
Heal my wounded, broken spirit,
Save me by Your grace.
Savior, Savior, hear my humble cry.

Let me at Your throne of mercy
Find a sweet relief;

Kneeling there in sweet contrition
Help my unbelief.
Savior, Savior, hear my humble cry.

You the spring of all my comfort,
More than life to me,
Whom have I on earth but Thee?
Whom in heaven but Thee?
Savior, Savior, hear my humble cry.

Fanny J. Crosby

The Refrain for the Vespers Lessons
Heal me, YAHWEH, and I shall be healed, save me and I shall saved, for you are my
praise.

Jeremiah 17:14

The Vespers Psalm   The LORD Is My Shepherd
The LORD is my shepherd;* I shall not be in want.

He makes me lie down in green pastures* and leads me beside still waters.

He revives my soul* and guides me along right pathways for his Name's sake.

Though I walk through the valley of the shadow of death, I shall fear no evil;* for
you are with me; your rod and your staff, they comfort me.

You spread a table before me in the presence of those who trouble me;* you have
anointed my head with oil, and my cup is running over.

Surely your goodness and mercy shall follow me all the days of my life,* and I will
dwell in the house of the LORD for ever.

Psalm 23

The Refrain
Heal me, YAHWEH, and I shall be healed, save me and I shall saved, for you are my
praise.

The Gloria

The Lord's Prayer

The Prayer Appointed for the Day
Almighty and everlasting God, by whose Spirit the whole body of your faithful
people is governed and sanctified: Receive my supplications and prayers, which

I offer before you for all members of your holy Church, that in our vocations and ministries we may truly and devoutly serve you; through our Lord and Savior Jesus Christ, who lives and reigns with you, in the unity of the Holy Spirit, one God, now and forever. *Amen.*

The Concluding Prayer of the Church

O merciful Creator, your hand is open wide to satisfy the needs of every living creature: Make me always thankful for your loving providence; and grant that remembering the account I must one day give, I may be a faithful steward of your good gifts; through Jesus Christ our Lord, who with you and the Holy Spirit lives and reigns, one God, for ever and ever. *Amen.*

The Office of Compline   To Be Observed Before Retiring

The Call to Prayer

May the Lord Almighty grant me and those I love a peaceful night and a perfect end. *Amen.*

The Request for Presence

Our help is in the Name of the Lord; the maker of heaven and earth.

The Greeting

Almighty God, my heavenly Father, I have sinned against you, through my own fault in thought, and word, and deed, in what I have done and what I have left undone. For the sake of your Son our Lord Jesus Christ, forgive me all my offenses; and grant that I may serve you in newness of life, to the glory of your Name. *Amen.*

The Reading

My God, let me remember and confess with gratitude to you your mercies over me. Let my bones be steeped in your love, and let them say to you, "Who is like you, LORD?" *(Ps 35:10)* "You have loosed my bonds of affliction. I will sacrifice a thank offering to you." *(Ps 115:16–17)* . . . And all who worship you, when they hear these things, will say, "Praise be to his glorious name forever; may the whole earth be filled with his glory." *(Ps 72:19)*

St. Augustine (ca. 410 CE), The Confessions, translated by Robert J. Edmonson, CJ

The Gloria

The Psalm   LORD, I Am Your Servant; You Have
                                 Freed Me from My Bonds

LORD, I am your servant;* I am your servant and the child of your handmaid; you
    have freed me from my bonds.
I will offer you the sacrifice of thanksgiving* and call upon the Name of the LORD.
I will fulfill my vows to the LORD* in the presence of all his people,
In the courts of the LORD's house,* in the midst of you, O Jerusalem. Hallelujah!

Psalm 116:14–17

The Gloria

The Small Verse

Into your hands, O Lord, I commend my spirit; For you have redeemed me, O Lord,
    O God of truth. Keep me, O Lord, as the apple of your eye; Hide me under the
    shadow of your wings.

The Lord's Prayer

The Petition

Keep watch, dear Lord, with those who work, or watch, or weep this night, and give
    your angels charge over those who sleep. Tend the sick, Lord Christ; give rest to
    the weary, bless the dying, soothe the suffering, pity the afflicted, shield the
    joyous; and all for your love's sake. *Amen.*

The Final Thanksgiving

Lord, you now have set your servant free to go in peace as you have promised; for
    these eyes of mine have seen the Savior, whom you have prepared for all the
    world to see: a Light to enlighten the nations, and the glory of your people Israel.
    Glory to the Father, and to the Son, and to the Holy Spirit: as it was in the
    beginning, is now, and ever more shall be. *Amen.*

SATURDAY

The Office of Midnight — To Be Observed on the Hour or Half Hour
Between 10:30 p.m. ✧ and 1:30 a.m.

The Call to Prayer
I will call upon the LORD,* and so shall I be saved from my enemies.

Psalm 18:3

The Request for Presence
O LORD, let my prayer be set forth in your sight as incense,* the lifting up of my
hands as the evening sacrifice.

Psalm 141:2, adapted

The Greeting
Our Father, may Your will be done on earth as in Heaven.

The Canticle   *The Second Song of Isaiah*
Quaerite Dominum

Seek the Lord while he wills to be found;*
    call upon him when he draws near.
Let the wicked forsake their ways*
    and the evil ones their thoughts;
And let them turn to the Lord, and he will have compassion,*
    and to our God, for he will richly pardon.
For my thoughts are not your thoughts,*
    nor your ways my ways, says the Lord.
For as the heavens are higher than the earth,*
    so are my ways higher than your ways, and my thoughts than your thoughts.
or as rain and snow fall from the heavens*
    and return not again, but water the earth,
Bringing forth life and giving growth,*
    seed for sowing and bread for eating,
So is my word that goes forth from my mouth;*
    it will not return to me empty;
But it will accomplish that which I have purposed,*
    and prosper in that for which I sent it.

Isaiah 55:6–11

The Psalm   ***God Girds Me About with Strength***

You, O LORD, are my lamp;* my God, you make my darkness bright.

With you I will break down an enclosure;* with the help of my God I will scale any
    wall.

As for God, his ways are perfect; the words of the LORD are tried in the fire;* he is a
    shield to all who trust in him.

For who is God, but the LORD?* who is the Rock, except our God?

It is God who girds me about with strength* and makes my way secure.

He makes me sure-footed like a deer* and lets me stand firm on the heights.

Psalm 18:29–34

The Gloria

The Small Verse

And he answered them, "Go and tell John what you have seen and heard: the blind
    receive their sight, the lame walk, lepers are cleansed, and the deaf hear, the
    dead are raised up, the poor have good news preached to them. And blessed is he
    who takes no offense at me."

Luke 7:22–23

The Final Thanksgiving

I will greatly rejoice in the LORD, my soul shall exult in my God; for he has
    clothed me with the garments of salvation, he has covered me with the robe
    of righteousness, as a bridegroom decks himself with a garland, and as a bride
    adorns herself with her jewels.

Isaiah 61:10

The Petition

May the Lord GOD, father of all mercy, grant us who dwell here a peaceful night and
    a perfect end. *Amen.*

Office of the Night Watch   **To Be Observed on the Hour or Half Hour Between 1:30 and 4:30 a.m.**

The Call to Prayer

Behold now, bless the LORD, all you servants of the LORD,* you that stand by night in the house of the LORD.

Lift up your hands in the holy place and bless the LORD;* the LORD who made heaven and earth bless you out of Zion.

Psalm 134

The Request for Presence

O God, come to my assistance.

O Lord, make haste to help me.

The Greeting

Who is like you, LORD God of hosts?* O mighty LORD, your faithfulness is all around you.

Psalm 89:8

The Refrain for the Night Watch

Happy are they who have not walked in the counsel of the wicked,* nor lingered in the way of sinners, nor sat in the seats of the scornful!

Their delight is in the law of the LORD,* and they meditate on his law day and night.

Psalm 1:1–2

The Psalm   *O LORD, Teach Me Your Paths*

To you, O LORD, I lift up my soul; my God, I put my trust in you;* let me not be humiliated, nor let my enemies triumph over me.

Let none who look to you be put to shame;* let the treacherous be disappointed in their schemes.

Show me your ways, O LORD,* and teach me your paths.

Lead me in your truth and teach me,* for you are the God of my salvation; in you have I trusted all the day long.

Psalm 25:1–4

The Refrain

Happy are they who have not walked in the counsel of the wicked,* nor lingered in
the way of sinners, nor sat in the seats of the scornful!
Their delight is in the law of the LORD,* and they meditate on his law day and night.

A Reading

Therefore, if you would stand and not fall, cease never in your intent, but beat
evermore on this cloud of unknowing that is betwixt you and your God with a
sharp dart of longing love, and be loathe to think on anything less than God, and
go not forth from that exercise for anything that happens. For this only is the
work that destroys the root and ground of sin.

The Cloud of Unknowing (14th c), Anonymous

The Refrain

Happy are they who have not walked in the counsel of the wicked,* nor lingered in
the way of sinners, nor sat in the seats of the scornful!
Their delight is in the law of the LORD,* and they meditate on his law day and night.

The Litany

From all evil and wickedness; from sin; from the crafts and assaults of the devil;
and from everlasting damnation,

Good Lord, deliver me.

From all blindness of heart; from pride, vainglory, and hypocrisy; from envy, hatred,
and malice; and from all want of charity,

Good Lord, deliver me.

From all inordinate and sinful affections; and from all the deceits of the world, the
flesh, and the devil,

Good Lord, deliver me.

From all false doctrine, heresy, and schism; from hardness of heart, and contempt of
your Word and commandment,

Good Lord, deliver me.

By the mystery of your holy Incarnation; by your holy Nativity and submission to
the Law; by your Baptism, Fasting, and Temptation,

Good Lord, deliver me.

In all time of tribulation; in all time of prosperity; in the hour of death, and in the
day of judgment,

Good Lord, deliver me.

The Thanksgiving

Lord, you now have set your servant free to go in peace as you have promised; for
these eyes of mine have seen the Savior whom you have prepared for all the
world to see: A Light to enlighten the nations, and the glory of your people
Israel. *Amen.*

Nunc Dimittis

The Final Petition

Now guide me waking, O Lord, and guard me sleeping; that awake I may watch with
Christ, and asleep, I may rest in peace. *Amen.*

ॐ

The Office of Dawn   **To Be Observed on the Hour or Half Hour**
Between 4:30 and 7:30 a.m.

The Call to Prayer

Hallelujah! Praise the LORD, O my soul!* I will praise the LORD as long as I live; I
will sing praises to my God while I have my being.

Psalm 146:1

The Request for Presence

My soul waits for the LORD, more than watchmen for the morning,* more than
watchmen for the morning.

Psalm 130:5

The Greeting

Glory be to the Father, and the Son, and the Holy Spirit.
As it was in the beginning, it is now
And ever shall be, world without end. *Amen.*

Gloria Patri

The Hymn

O strength and stay upholding all creation,
Who ever does Himself unmoved abide,

yet day by day the light in due gradation
from hour to hour through all its changes guide;
Grant to life's day a calm, unclouded ending,
an eve untouched by shadows of decay,
the brightness of a holy deathbed blending
with dawning glories of the eternal day.

Hear us, O Father, gracious and forgiving
and You, O Christ, the coeternal Word,
Who with the Holy Spirit by all things living
now and to endless ages are adored. *Amen.*

St. Ambrose, translated by J. Ellerton and F. J. A. Hort

The Psalm   The Lord Sends His Command to the Earth

The LORD sends out his command to the earth,* and his word runs very swiftly.
He gives snow like wool;* he scatters hoarfrost like ashes.
He scatters his hail like bread crumbs;* who can stand against his cold?
He sends forth his word and melts them;* he blows with his wind, and the waters
    flow.

Psalm 147:16–19

The Gloria in Excelsis

Glory to God in the highest, and on earth peace to people of good will.
    We praise you.
    We bless you.
    We adore you.
    We glorify you.
We give thanks to you for your great glory.

The Small Verse

There is one body and one Spirit, just as you were called to the one hope that
    belongs to your call, one Lord, one faith, one baptism, one God and Father of us
    all, who is above all and through all and in all. But grace was given to each of us
    according to the measure of Christ's gift.

Ephesians 4:4–7

The Lord's Prayer

The Final Blessing

May the LORD bless us and keep us and cause His face to shine upon us from this
day forth and forever more. *Amen.*

჻

The Morning Office **To Be Observed on the Hour or Half Hour**
Between 6 and 9 a.m.

The Call to Prayer

Let the name of the LORD be blessed,* from this time forth for evermore.
From the rising of the sun to its going down* let the Name of the LORD be praised.

Psalm 113:2–3

The Request for Presence

Let my cry come before you, O LORD;* give me understanding according to your
word.
Let my supplication come before you;* deliver me according to your promise.

Psalm 119:169–170

The Greeting

I love you, O LORD my strength,* O LORD my stronghold, my crag, and my haven.
My God, my rock in whom I put my trust,* my shield, the horn of my salvation, and
my refuge; you are worthy of praise.

Psalm 18:1–2

The Refrain for the Morning Lessons

For who is God, but the LORD?* who is the Rock except your God?

Psalm 18:32

A Reading

Jesus said: 'Anyone who wishes to be a follower of mine must renounce self; he
must take up his cross and follow me. Whoever wants to save his life will lose it,
but whoever loses his life for my sake will find it. What will anyone gain by

winning the whole world at the cost of his life? Or what can he give to buy his life back?'

Matthew 16:24–26

The Refrain
For who is God, but the LORD?* who is the Rock except your God?

The Morning Psalm   The LORD Is My Strength and My Shield
Blessed is the LORD!* for he has heard the voice of my prayer.
The LORD is my strength and my shield;* my heart trusts in him, and I have been helped;
Therefore my heart dances for joy,* and in my song will I praise him.
The LORD is the strength of his people,* a safe refuge for his anointed.
Save your people and bless your inheritance;* shepherd them and carry them for ever.

Psalm 28:7–11

The Refrain
For who is God, but the LORD?* who is the Rock except your God?

The Gloria

The Lord's Prayer

The Prayer Appointed for the Day
Almighty God, who after the creation of the world rested from all your works and sanctified a day of rest for all your creatures: Grant that I, putting away all earthly anxieties, may be duly prepared for the service of public worship, and grant as well that my Sabbath upon earth may be a preparation for the eternal rest promised to your people in heaven, through Jesus Christ, our Lord. *Amen.*

The Concluding Prayer of the Church
Lord God, almighty and everlasting Father, you have brought me in safety to the beginning of this day: Preserve me with your mighty power, that I may not fall into sin, nor be overcome by adversity; and in all I do, direct me to the fulfilling of your purposes; through Jesus Christ my Lord. *Amen.*

The Midday Office　　　　　**To Be Observed on the Hour or Half Hour Between 11 a.m. and 2 p.m.**

The Call to Prayer
Blessed be the LORD, the God of Israel, from everlasting and to everlasting;* and let
　　all the people say, "Amen!"

Psalm 106:48

The Request for Presence
Show us your mercy, O LORD,* and grant us your salvation.

Psalm 85:7

The Greeting
The eyes of all wait upon you, O LORD.*

Psalm 145:16

The Refrain for the Midday Lessons
Your kingdom is an everlasting kingdom;* your dominion endures throughout
　　all ages.

Psalm 145:13

A Reading
Seek the LORD while he is present, call to him while he is close at hand. Let the
　　wicked abandon their ways and the evil their thoughts: let them return to the
　　LORD, who will take pity on them, and to our God, for he will freely forgive. For
　　my thoughts are not your thoughts, nor my ways your ways. This is the word of
　　the LORD. But as the heavens are high above the earth, so are my ways above
　　your ways and my thoughts above your thoughts.

Isaiah 55:6–9

The Refrain
Your kingdom is an everlasting kingdom;* your dominion endures throughout
　　all ages.

The Midday Psalm　　　　　*Those Who Await His Gracious Favor*
He covers the heavens with clouds* and prepares rain for the earth;
He makes grass to grow upon the mountains* and green plants to serve mankind.
He provides food for flocks and herds* and for the young ravens when they cry.

He is not impressed by the might of a horse;* he has no pleasure in the strength of a man;

But the LORD has pleasure in those who fear him,* in those who await his gracious favor.

Psalm 147:8–12

The Refrain

Your kingdom is an everlasting kingdom;* your dominion endures throughout all ages.

The Gloria

The Lord's Prayer

The Prayer Appointed for the Day

Almighty God, who after the creation of the world rested from all your works and sanctified a day of rest for all your creatures: Grant that I, putting away all earthly anxieties, may be duly prepared for the service of public worship, and grant as well that my Sabbath upon earth may be a preparation for the eternal rest promised to your people in heaven, through Jesus Christ, our Lord. *Amen.*

The Concluding Prayer of the Church

Lord Jesus Christ, you said to your apostles, "Peace I give to you; my own peace I leave with you:" Regard not my sins, but my faith, and give me a place in the peace and unity of that heavenly City, where with the Father and the Holy Spirit you live and reign now and forever. *Amen.*

ॐ

The Vespers Office   **To Be Observed on the Hour or Half Hour Between 5 and 8 p.m.**

The Call to Prayer

We will bless the LORD,* from this time forth for evermore.

Psalm 115:18

The Request for Presence

Answer me when I call, O God, defender of my cause;* you set me free when I am
hard-pressed; have mercy on me and hear my prayer.

Psalm 4:1

The Greeting

The LORD lives! Blessed is my Rock!* Exalted is the God of my salvation!

Psalm 18:46

The Hymn

Dear Lord and father of mankind,
Forgive our foolish ways;
Reclothe us in our rightful mind;
In purer lives Your service find,
In deeper reverence praise.

Drop Your still dews of quietness.
Til all our strivings cease;
Take from our souls the strain and stress,
And let our ordered lives confess
The beauty of Your peace.

Breathe through the heats of our desire
Your coolness and Your balm;
Let sense be dumb, let flesh retire;
Speak through the earthquake, wind, and fire,
O still small voice of calm!

In simple trust like theirs who heard,
Beside the Syrian sea,
The gracious calling of the Lord.
Let us, like them, without a word,
Rise up and follow Thee.

John G. Whittier

The Refrain for the Vespers Lessons

Blessed be God, who has not rejected my prayer,* nor withheld his love from me.

Psalm 66:18

The Vespers Psalm   Rejoice in the LORD

You are my hiding-place; you preserve me from trouble;* you surround me with
    shouts of deliverance.

"I will instruct you and teach you in the way that you should go;* I will guide you
    with my eye.

Do not be like horse or mule, which have no understanding;* who must be fitted
    with bit and bridle, or else they will not stay near you."

Great are the tribulations of the wicked;* but mercy embraces those who trust in the
    LORD.

Be glad, you righteous, and rejoice in the LORD;* shout for joy, all who are true of
    heart.

Psalm 32:8–12

The Refrain

Blessed be God, who has not rejected my prayer,* nor withheld his love from me.

The Gloria

The Lord's Prayer

The Prayer Appointed for the Day

Almighty God, who after the creation of the world rested from all your works and
    sanctified a day of rest for all your creatures: Grant that I, putting away all
    earthly anxieties, may be duly prepared for the service of public worship, and
    grant as well that my Sabbath upon earth may be a preparation for the eternal
    rest promised to your people in heaven, through Jesus Christ, our Lord. *Amen.*

The Concluding Prayer of the Church

O God, the source of light: Shed forth your unending day upon all of us who watch
    for you, that our lips may praise you, our lives may bless you, and our worship
    may give you glory; through Jesus Christ our Lord. *Amen.*

The Office of Compline　　　　To Be Observed Before Retiring

The Call to Prayer
May the Lord Almighty grant me and those I love a peaceful night and a perfect end.
Amen.

The Request for Presence
Our help is in the Name of the Lord; the maker of heaven and earth.

The Greeting
Almighty God, my heavenly Father, I have sinned against you, through my own fault
in thought, and word, and deed, in what I have done and what I have left undone.
For the sake of your Son our Lord Jesus Christ, forgive me all my offenses; and
grant that I may serve you in newness of life, to the glory of your Name. *Amen.*

The Reading
You know, I am sure, that the kingdom of heaven is promised and given by the Lord
only to the poor: for he who loves temporal things loses the fruit of love. Such a
person cannot serve God and Mammon, for either the one is loved and the other
hated, or the one is served and the other despised.

You also know that one who is clothed cannot fight with another who is naked,
because he is more quickly thrown who gives his adversary a chance to get hold
of him; and that one who lives in the glory of earth cannot rule with Christ in
heaven.

St. Clare of Assisi, First Letter to Blessed Agnes of Prague (ca. 1234 CE)

The Gloria

The Psalm　　　　　　　　　　*Put not Your Trust in Rulers*
Put not your trust in rulers, nor in any child of earth,* for there is no help in them.
When they breathe their last, they return to earth,* and in that day their thoughts
perish.
Happy are they who have the God of Jacob for their help!* whose hope is in the
LORD their God;
The LORD shall reign for ever,* your God, O Zion, throughout all generations.
Hallelujah!

Psalm 146:2–4, 9

The Gloria

The Small Verse
Into your hands, O Lord, I commend my spirit; For you have redeemed me, O Lord, O God of truth. Keep me, O Lord, as the apple of your eye; Hide me under the shadow of your wings.

The Lord's Prayer

The Petition
Keep watch, dear Lord, with those who work, or watch, or weep this night, and give your angels charge over those who sleep. Tend the sick, Lord Christ; give rest to the weary, bless the dying, soothe the suffering, pity the afflicted, shield the joyous; and all for your love's sake. *Amen.*

The Final Thanksgiving
Lord, you now have set your servant free to go in peace as you have promised; for these eyes of mine have seen the Savior, whom you have prepared for all the world to see: a Light to enlighten the nations, and the glory of your people Israel. Glory to the father, and to the Son, and to the Holy Spirit: as it was in the beginning, is now, and ever more shall be. *Amen.*

TRADITIONAL
SEASONAL
AND
OCCASIONAL
PRAYERS

Traditional Prayers

Anima Christi
Soul of Christ, sanctify me,
Body of Christ, save me,
Blood of Christ, flood me,
Water from the side of Christ, wash me.
O good Jesu, hear me,
Within your wounds hide me,
Suffer me not to be separated from you,
From the malicious enemy defend me,
In the hour of my death call me,
And bid me come to you,
That with your saints I may praise you,
For ever and ever. *Amen.*

Collect for Purity
Almighty God, to whom all hearts are open, all desires known, and from whom no
secrets are hidden: cleanse the thoughts of our hearts by the inspiration of your
Holy Spirit, that we may perfectly love you, and worthily magnify your holy
name; through Christ our Lord. *Amen.*

The Angelus
The angel of the Lord brought tidings to Mary:
And she conceived by the Holy Ghost.

Hail, Mary, full of grace, the Lord is with you:
Blessed are you among women, and blessed is
the fruit of your womb, Jesus.
Behold the handmaid of the Lord:
Be it unto me according to your word.

Hail, Mary, full of grace, the Lord is with you:
Blessed are you among women, and blessed is
the fruit of your womb, Jesus.

And the Word was made flesh:
And dwelt among us.

Hail, Mary, full of grace, the Lord is with you:
Blessed are you among women, and blessed is
the fruit of your womb, Jesus.

Pray for us, O holy Mother of God:
That we may be made worthy of the promises of Christ.

We beseech you, O Lord, to pour your grace into our heart that as we have known
the incarnation of your Son Jesus Christ by the message of the angel, so by his
cross and passion we may be brought to the glory of his resurrection, through the
same Christ our Lord. *Amen.*

Veni Sancte Spiritus
Come, O holy Paraclete,
And from your celestial seat
Send your light and brilliancy:
Father of the poor, draw near;
Giver of gifts, be here;
Come, the soul's true radiancy.

Come, of the comforters the best,
Of the soul the sweetest guest,
Come in toil refreshingly;
You in labor rest most sweet,
You in shadow from the heat,
Comfort in adversity.

O light, most pure and blest,
Shine within the inmost breast
Of your faithful company.
Where you are not, man has nought;
Every holy deed and thought
Comes from your divinity.

What is soiled, you make pure;
What is wounded, work its cure;
What is parched, fructify;
What is rigid, gently bend;
What is frozen, gently tend;
Straighten what goes erringly.

Fill your faithful, who confide
In your power to guard and guide,
With your sevenfold mystery.
Here they grace and virtue send;
Grant salvation in the end,
And in heaven felicity.

Adapted from the Essential Book of Catholic Prayers

St. Patrick's Breastplate
I bind unto myself this day
the power of God to hold and lead,
his eye to watch, his might to stay,
his ear to harken to my need:
the wisdom of my God to teach,
his hand to guide, his shield to ward:
the word of God to give me speech,
his heavenly host to be my guard.

Christ be with me, Christ before me,
Christ behind me, Christ deep within me,
Christ below me, Christ above me,
Christ at my right hand, Christ at my left hand,
Christ as I lie down, Christ as I arise,
Christ as I stand,
Christ in the heart of everyone who thinks of me,
Christ in the mouth of everyone who speaks of me,
Christ in every eye that sees me,
Christ in every ear that hears me.

translated by Cecil F. Alexander

The Prayer of St. Francis
Lord, make me an instrument of your peace:
    where there is hatred let me sow love,
    where there is injury let me sow pardon,
    where there is doubt let me sow faith,
    where there is despair let me sow hope,
    where there is darkness let me give light,
    where there is sadness let me give joy.

O divine master, grant that I may
    not try to be comforted, but to comfort,
    not try to be understood, but to understand,
    not try to be loved, but to love.

For it is in giving that we receive,
    it is in forgiving that we are forgiven,
    and it is in dying that we are born to eternal life. *Amen.*

Salvator Mundi
Jesus, Savior of the world,
    come to us in your mercy:
we look to you to save and help us.

By your cross and your life laid down,
    you set your people free:
we look to you to save and help us.

When they were ready to perish
    you saved your disciples:
we look to you to come to our help.

In the greatness of your mercy,
    loose us from our chains:
forgive the sins of all your people.

Make yourself known
    as our savior and mighty deliverer:
Save and help us that we may praise you.

Come now and dwell with us, Lord Christ Jesus:
    hear our prayer and be with us always.

And when you come in your glory:
    make us to be one with you
and to share the life of your kingdom. *Amen*

Seasonal Prayers

Advent

Almighty God, give us grace to cast away the works of darkness, and put on the armor of light, now in the time of this mortal life in which your Son Jesus Christ came to visit us in great humility; that in the last day, when he shall come again in his glorious majesty to judge both the living and the dead, we may rise to life immortal; through him who lives and reigns with you and the Holy Spirit, one God, now and for ever. *Amen.*

Christmas

O God, you make us glad with the yearly festival of the birth of your only Son Jesus Christ: Grant that we, who joyfully receive him as our Redeemer, may with sure confidence behold him when he comes to be our Judge; who lives and reigns with you and the Holy Spirit, one God, now and for ever. *Amen.*

Epiphany

O God, by the leading of a star you manifested your only Son to the peoples of the earth; Lead us, who know you now by faith, to your presence, where we may see your glory face to face; through Jesus Christ our Lord, who lives and reigns with you and the Holy Spirit, one God, now and for ever. *Amen.*

Lent

Almighty and everlasting God, you hate nothing you have made and forgive the sins of all who are penitent: Create and make in us new and contrite hearts, that we, worthily lamenting our sins and acknowledging our wretchedness, may obtain of you, the God of all mercy, perfect remission and forgiveness; through Jesus Christ our Lord, who lives and reigns with you and the Holy Spirit, one God, now and for ever. *Amen.*

Palm Sunday

Almighty God, whose most dear Son went not up to joy but first he suffered pain, and entered not into glory before he was crucified: Mercifully grant that we, walking in the way of the cross, may find it none other than the way of life and peace; through Jesus Christ our Lord, who lives and reigns with you and the Holy Spirit, one God, now and for ever. *Amen.*

Good Friday

Almighty God, we pray you graciously to behold this your family, for whom our Lord Jesus Christ was willing to be betrayed, and given into the hands of sinners, and to suffer death upon the cross; who now lives and reigns with you and the Holy Spirit, one God, now and for ever. *Amen.*

Holy Saturday

O God, Creator of heaven and earth: Grant that, as the crucified body of your dear Son was laid in the tomb and rested on this holy Sabbath, so we may await with him the coming of the third day, and rise with him to newness of life; who now lives and reigns with you and the Holy Spirit, one God, now and for ever. *Amen.*

Easter

O God, who for our redemption gave your only-begotten Son to the death of the cross, and by his glorious resurrection delivered us from the power of our enemy: Grant us so to die daily to sin, that we may evermore live with him in the joy of his resurrection; through Jesus Christ our Lord, who lives and reigns with you and the Holy Spirit, one God, in glory everlasting. *Amen.*

Ascension

Almighty God, whose blessed Son our Savior Jesus Christ ascended far above all heavens that he might fill all things: Mercifully give us faith to perceive that, according to his promise, he abides with his Church on earth, even to the end of the ages; through Jesus Christ our Lord, who lives and reigns with you and the Holy Spirit, one God, now and for ever. *Amen.*

Pentecost

Almighty God, on this day you opened the way of eternal life to every race and nation by the promised gift of your Holy Spirit: Shed abroad this gift throughout the world by the preaching of the Gospel, that it may reach to the ends of the earth; through Jesus Christ our Lord, who lives and reigns with you and the Holy Spirit, one God, now and for ever. *Amen.*

All Saints

Almighty God, you have knit together your elect in one communion and fellowship in the mystical body of your Son Christ our Lord: Give us grace so to follow

120

your blessed saints in all virtuous and godly living, that we may come to those ineffable joys that you have prepared for those who truly love you; through Jesus Christ our Lord, who lives and reigns with you and the Holy Spirit, one God, now and for ever. *Amen.*

Thanksgiving

Accept, O Lord, my thanks and praise for all that you have done for us. I thank you for the splendor of the whole creation, for the beauty of this world, for the wonder of life, and for the mystery of love.

I thank you for the blessing of family and friends, and for the loving care that surrounds us on every side.

I thank you also for those disappointments and failures that lead us to acknowledge our dependence on you alone.

Above all, I thank you for your Son Jesus Christ; for the truth of his Word and the example of his life; for his steadfast obedience, by which he overcame temptation; for his dying, through which he overcame death; and for his rising to life again, in which we are raised to the life of your kingdom.

Grant me the gift of your Spirit, that I may know Christ and make him known; and through him, at all times and in all places, may give thanks to you in all things. *Amen.*

Occasional Prayers

For A Saint's Day

O Almighty God, who by your Holy Spirit has made us one with your saints in
heaven and on earth: Grant that in my earthly pilgrimage I may ever be
supported by this fellowship of love and prayer, and may know myself to be
surrounded by their witness to your power and mercy. I ask this for the sake of
Jesus Christ, in whom all our intercessions are acceptable through the Spirit, and
who lives and reigns for ever and ever. *Amen.*

For Those About To Be Married

O God, you have so consecrated the covenant of marriage that in it is represented
the spiritual unity between Christ and his Church: Send therefore your blessing
upon your servants (N & N), that they may so love, honor and cherish each other
in faithfulness and patience, in wisdom and true godliness, that their home may
be a haven of blessing and peace; through Jesus Christ our Lord, who lives and
reigns with you and the Holy Spirit, one God, now and for ever. *Amen.*

Upon the Birth or Adoption of a Child

O God, you have taught us through your blessed Son that whoever receives a little
child in the name of Christ receives Christ himself: I/We give you thanks for the
blessing you have bestowed upon this family by giving them a child. Confirm
their joy by a lively sense of your presence with them, and give them calm
strength and patient wisdom as they seek to bring this child to love all that is true
and noble, just and pure, lovable and gracious, excellent and admirable,
following the example of our Lord and Savor Jesus Christ. *Amen.*

In Time of Personal Illness

O God, the source of all health: So fill my heart with faith in your love. That with
calm expectancy I may make room for your power to possess me, and gracefully
accept your healing; through Jesus Christ our Lord. *Amen.*

For the Sick

Heavenly Father, Giver of life and health: Comfort and relieve your sick servants
and give your power of healing to those who minister to their needs, that those
(or Name) for whom my prayers are offered may be strengthened in his/her/their

distress and have sure knowledge of your loving care through Jesus Christ our Lord, who lives and reigns with you and the Holy Spirit, one God, now and for ever. *Amen*.

For the Dying (Adult)

O God, whose mercies cannot be numbered: Accept my prayers on behalf of your servant (Name) and grant him/her an entrance into the land of light and joy, in the fellowship of your saints; through Jesus Christ our Lord, who lives and reigns with you and the Holy Spirit, one God, now and for ever. *Amen.*

Into your hands, O merciful Savior, we commend your servant (N) Acknowledge, I humbly beseech you, a sheep of your own fold, a lamb of your own flock, a sinner of your own redeeming. Receive him/her/N into the arms of your mercy, into the blessed rest of everlasting peace, and into the glorious company of the saints in light. *Amen.*

For the Dying (Child)

O God, whose beloved Son took children into his arms and blessed them: Give us grace to entrust (Name) to your never failing care and love, and bring us all to your heavenly kingdom; through Jesus Christ Our Lord, who lives and reigns with you and the Holy Spirit, one God, now and for ever. *Amen.*

For Those Who Mourn

Most merciful God, whose wisdom is beyond our understanding: Deal graciously with (Name/s) in this time of grief. Surround all those who mourn now with your love, that he/she/they may not be overwhelmed by this loss, but may have confidence in your goodness, and strength to meet the days to come; through Jesus Christ our Lord. *Amen.*

List of Authors

Acknowledgments

The selection from *The Confessions* of St. Augustine is taken from *You Converted Me—The Confessions of St. Augustine*, Robert J. Edmonson, CJ, trans. Copyright 2006 by Paraclete Press. Used by permission.

HE—Psalm 119: 33–40 is taken from *This Holy Alphabet: A Cycle of 22 Lyric Poems from Psalm 119*. Margaret B. Ingraham. Copyright 2006, Margaret B. Ingraham. Used by permission.

Unless otherwise noted, all scripture selections are taken from *The Oxford Study Bible—Revised English Bible with the Apocrypha*. Copyright 1976 by Oxford University Press. Used by permission.

Unless otherwise noted, all prayers and psalms are selected or adapted from *The Book of Common Prayer* and are used by permission.